WASHINGTON STATE

PODEROSAS

CONVERSATIONS WITH EXTRAORDINARY, ORDINARY WOMEN

Lisette García, Ph.D.

For information about permissions to reproduce selections from this book,
translation rights, or to order bulk purchases, go to www.SunyataBooks.com

Edited by Barrett Martin
Cover art by Erin Currier
Author photo by Bliss Rowland
Book interior design by Barrett Martin
Book cover design by Juliana Um and Chadwick Shao

García, Lisette
Poderosas: Conversations With Extraordinary, Ordinary Women
ISBN 978-0-578-73088-2

1. Biography & Autobiography / Women

Printed in the U.S.A.
Distributed by Ingram

WWW.SUNYATABOOKS.COM
WWW.LISETTEGARCIA.COM

PODEROSAS

CONVERSATIONS WITH EXTRAORDINARY, ORDINARY WOMEN

This book is dedicated to all the women who found greatness within themselves, and for all the others who are still searching for it.

FOREWORD

Barrett Martin: The Power of Feminine Wisdom

"A woman's guess is much more accurate than a man's certainty."
                                                    -Rudyard Kipling

All of my greatest teachers have been women.

It's not because I didn't have great male teachers as well—I certainly did, many of them artists, warriors, and men of great honor and skill. However, in matters of spiritual understanding and personal guidance, it was my female teachers and mentors who seemed to have the greatest insights into the nature of our existence, our understanding of the natural world, and our relationships to each other. These women had the ability to convey those most important teachings, clearly and concisely, even though they varied widely in their spiritual traditions. They spanned many different periods of my life, and they ranged from a Cherokee healer who gave me my first Indigenous initiations, to a Zen master who gave me my first ordination in Buddhism, to a powerful Shipibo Shaman who I worked with in the Peruvian Amazon, to an academic advisor who gave me profound wisdom during a critical period in my professional life.

My own mother and grandmother have both been teachers to me, as is my wife, Dr. Lisette García. Not only is Lisette a powerful teacher, she is also a scholar of psychology and Buddhist philosophy, and she is the spearpoint of this book. She is the guide who takes the reader through the most important facets of deep, feminine wisdom.

So if any of you are wondering why a man's voice is appearing in the foreword of a book that is essentially about the power of women, these are exactly the reasons: I am advocating for the embrace of female wisdom, power, and leadership in the United States and around the world. This is also why I hope that many different types of men will read this book, and in doing so, educate themselves on the immense power of the feminine perspective. This is what the great martial artist, Bruce Lee, was talking about when he described the best way to approach a difficult situation—"Be like water." This is the Yin principle, the feminine principle, and it's ability to overcome things that the masculine cannot.

All of the women interviewed in this book were great teachers to both Lisette and me, so to encapsulate the wide range of their stories and wisdom, we have used a methodology akin to conversational storytelling, where Lisette asks a series of questions, which evolves into deeper questions as the conversations unfold. Since I participated in many essential aspects of the book, including the recording, editing, and design, Lisette wanted my voice in here too. Thus, in a few of the stories, I introduce the women who were highly influential on my development, and in some cases have been my teachers for over 25 years. I describe their role in my life, including some of the ceremonies they taught me, and I ask a few questions within the conversations, to show my engagement with their teachings.

This is also a way to show why participating with, and understanding feminine wisdom, should be an integral part of every man's spiritual, emotional, and intellectual development. All of this is a statement on the polarization that has been created in the power struggles of the current, male-dominated world, and why we must return to a state of balance. Thus, I begin this very daunting task by remembering an ancient Celtic myth, which I think most people are familiar with.

When Arthur Pendragon pulled the supernatural sword, Excalibur, from the Sacred Stone, it was seen as a divine event which, from that moment onward, granted Arthur his kingship and rule over the land. "The king and the land are one" it was proclaimed, but what is often forgotten in this great myth, is that Excalibur was originally placed in the stone by Merlin, after he, the Great Master Of The Old Ways, received it from The Lady Of The Lake. It was She, the Great Mother, imbued with all the magic and wisdom of the Earth, who granted Her power to Merlin, who then forwarded it on to Arthur. It then became Arthur and Merlin's mutual duty to protect everyone in the land with the feminine power of that sword, the most important of which was the Divine Feminine, because it was She who granted them Her magic in the first place.

You see, all true power emanates from the feminine, from the divine, and it is granted to both men and women who are deemed virtuous enough to wield it. This power does not necessarily come from noble birth, indeed, most so-called nobles are often the most corrupt and incompetent at wielding power, as many current royals have demonstrated. The sword is simply a metaphor for that divine, feminine magic, manifested as a sword of discriminating wisdom, and then temporarily granted to a person of righteous intent.

And like Arthur, after he was mortally wounded in battle and taken to the island of Avalon to become immortalized, Excalibur was duly returned to the Lady Of The Lake until England (a metaphor for the Earth) is threatened again. At that point, and I believe that time is now, The Great Lady will return to call upon Her mighty warriors, to bestow Her divine powers unto them once again.

We see this archetypical pattern of divine feminine power all over the world and throughout history, where women either grant or rescind their power to heroes, sometimes taking that power unto themselves as they transform entire nations.

The Great Mother of all the African Orishas, Yemoja, lives in the deepest depths of the ocean, where she hides all of the secrets of Earth and Time in the folds of her skirt—secrets which are only revealed to the most worthy. She is the original Ocean Goddess, and from her springs all life and all wisdom. Her daughters, Oya and Osun, rule the realms of wind and storms, and fresh waters respectively, and these three women are the archetypes from which all other goddesses follow.

Greek goddesses anointed their human progeny with superpowers that helped them defeat monsters and tyrants on Earth, and the Oracles of Delphi prophesized for Greek warriors before they engaged in history-changing battles.

White Buffalo Calf Woman gave the Lakota tribes of North America their sacred ceremonies, which in turn made the Lakota the fiercest warriors in American history—they defeated the US Cavalry in almost every engagement.

The famed Shipibo Shamans of the Peruvian Amazon still practice their ancient song-healing techniques, handed down from grandmother to granddaughter, and feminine wisdom still presides over the Indigenous societies throughout the Amazon River Basin.

The Polynesia warrior-god, Maui, was given supernatural powers by his grandmother who gifted him with magic, and matriarchal traditions still rule the Polynesian cultures of Hawaii, Samoa, Tahiti, New Zealand, and the islands scattered across the Pacific Ocean.

Cleopatra and the queens of African nations ruled huge swaths of the African continent, and the most powerful and successful pirate in that hemisphere was a Chinese female sea captain named Cheng I Sao. Cheng commanded over two thousand ships, with tens of thousands of sailors at her command, and she ruled the Indian and western Pacific Oceans, engaging with, and defeating European navies. When she retired, she was one of the wealthiest women in history.

Joan of Arc literally picked up a sword to lead the French army to victory when she drove the English out of France, and one hundred years later, Queen Elizabeth I united England, when she erased the globally marauding Spanish Armada. Shortly thereafter, Catherine The Great united Russia, thus making it a respected European power, until it was eventually corrupted again by the gangsterism of modern Russia.

In the modern world, some of Europe's most prosperous countries are led by female prime ministers and presidents, and in the United States, female political leaders are proving to be far more competent and effective than most of their male peers. At some point, hopefully in the near future, the United States will finally elect a female president, and it's important to remember that this possibility of a Madam President was actually seeded a long time ago, by Indigenous women in the Great Lakes region of North America.

In that area, and over 250 years ago, there existed a huge federation of Indigenous nations, who decided all matters of people and state, and this is where the original American democracy began. It was called The League Of The Iroquois, and it encompassed the Great Lakes, New England, and Canada for centuries. It consisted of five Indigenous nations, those being the Mohawk, the Onondaga, the Oneida, the Cayuga, and the Seneca.

Three of the American Founders—Benjamin Franklin, John Adams, and Thomas Jefferson, sent emissaries to the League, to learn as much as they could about this Indigenous system of democracy, as they struggled to create a new political system for the fledgling American republic.

It was in The League Of The Iroquois where they discovered the best model for a system of self-governance, combined with the tenets of European Enlightenment philosophy, which had shaped their Western minds so powerfully.

As it worked, the League Of The Iroquois would elect a *Sachem* for each Indigenous district, a Sachem being the equivalent to what we might call a Senator. If the women of a given district decided that their particular Sachem wasn't doing their best in representing the people justly, they had the authority to revoke that power and elect a new Sachem. That's the part we need to remember now—the part about the women deciding who will be allowed to wield power, and who should have it taken away.

The most egregious flaw in the American Founder's vision of democracy, is that they neglected to include the League's primary tenet, which was the women's right to grant or rescind power, the right to maintain peace between the tribes, and even the right to declare war if necessary. This was the Founders' greatest folly, and it's one that haunts our nation to this day—leaving women and minorities out of the power-granting process, and making it harder for them to have an equal voice in the democratic process.

The United States has a huge responsibility to bear in this matter, because our own Constitution is the template used by the vast majority of nations around the world. Those nations see our Constitution as an example of enlightened political management, even if at times, we have found ourselves in a crisis, perhaps caused by a particularly corrupt President, Judge, or group of Senators, and that's when the Constitution is supposed to work. Because of our relatively evolved approach to democracy and human rights, most of the world has taken notice of our example, thus to falter in these commitments, would be disastrous for the evolution of the United States and the entire world. This is especially true now, with the growing environmental crisis, an increase in authoritarianism, and the economic instability that the entire world is facing.

The women that Lisette interviewed for this book are as diverse as the cultures from which they came from, and as powerful as the archetypes they embody. They are Latina, Cherokee, Shipibo, Tlingit, Anglo American, African American, and mixed race, yet there is a remarkable similarity in the trajectories of their lives and their progressive worldviews, which are based on personal experience and deep wisdom.

In almost every example, the very challenges and setbacks they experienced as young women, were the very things that gave them their unique skills, visions, and professional motivations as their lives unfolded.

Their spiritual beliefs and philosophies range from ancient Buddhism, to Christianity, to Native American spiritual practices, to Amazonian shamanism, and various forms of progressive, social activism. They are doctors, university professors, traditional healers, spiritual advisors, shamans, martial artists, dancers, painters, writers, and sometimes several of these things all at once. These are women who have quietly worked in their own corner of the world to become empowered, indeed, *Poderosas*, which in the Spanish language means *Mighty Women*. They did not seek fame or notoriety, in fact, most of the women interviewed here are, for the most part, non-famous. Yet, through their supreme efforts and skill, their sphere of influence changed the world much for the better, and in doing so, they became masters of their own destinies.

These are remarkable human beings, each of them with powerful teachings and personal experiences that need to be shared with the world. Each story received the final approval of the storyteller herself, and we feel that this is the most authentic, accurate, and honorable way to tell their stories— in their own words.

These stories are instilled with great wit and humor, and sometimes deep sadness too, because this is the nature of a life fully lived and fully realized. Our conversations took place in environments as diverse as the women themselves, and are indicative of their unique personalities. We spoke in places that ranged from a Texas barbeque, to a Lakota sweat lodge ceremony, to a longhouse in the Peruvian Amazon Rainforest, to a noisy New York restaurant, to a cozy home in the Alaskan Arctic, to a traditional Japanese Zendo, to a home on the Texas/Mexico border, to a Brooklyn artist's loft, to a pickup truck, speeding across the New Mexico desert.

However unusual the circumstances might be, the overriding themes that emerged throughout these stories, are that of fierce conviction to a personal path, and an urgency to address the state of the Earth's social, economic, and environmental crisis. Most notably, they speak about the collapse of the Earth's natural systems, which have analogs throughout society in our health, education, political, economic, and spiritual institutions, many of which are in parallel stages of collapse, or in some cases, renewal. All of this requires that we listen to the feminine voice of wisdom, that which can articulate most clearly how we can navigate and stabilize this very unsteady world.

Like all things in the universe, there is a balance-seeking mechanism at play, and with human beings, that mechanism is manifesting as an awakening consciousness in progressive people of all races and genders. Fortunately, the vast majority of people around the world are waking up to this movement, and they are saying that perhaps it's the women we should be listening to now, especially since the last 2,000 years of male-dominated patriarchy has brought us to the brink of environmental, economic, and cultural collapse.

Let us revisit the old traditions where women led the world in a more elegant, compassionate, and sustainable way. It is time for women to have their say again, now, just as they did in the League Of The Iroquois, and as they do in the countless Indigenous societies that still exist on Earth.

The following stories are for those Poderosas of the world, those Mighty Ones who make the Earth tremble and reverberate, every time they speak or take action on behalf of the marginalized, the unheard, and those who seek justice against the unjust.

Let's hear some of their stories now.

INTRODUCTION

Dr. Lisette García: Between Worlds

"There is no greater agony than bearing an untold story inside you."
— Maya Angelou

When something is out of balance, by definition, the outcome is disequilibrium. I have sought balance in every aspect of my life, with varying degrees of success, and this book is no exception. I could have written a book about women that excluded my husband, and why not—women are often excluded from conversations of great importance. If I did that, I feel I would be playing into the very polarization that I hope this book helps us move beyond. That's because my husband, Barrett Martin, is a feminist.

If it were up to Barrett, women would be running the world. "Men have already had their chance, and all we have proved is what a mess we can make of things," I've heard him espouse on more than one occasion. I don't know if I agree that women should run all aspects of the world, I merely want balance. It's akin to saying that I am not seeking reparations for how my people have been mistreated, I just want justice, I just want equal rights.

My relationship with my husband is one of my greatest achievements. This relationship would not be possible if he and I were looking for the other to make us happy. Our relationship works because we have both mindfully made efforts to be the best version of ourselves before we ever met. So when I say that the relationship is my greatest achievement, what I'm really saying is that it is the result of a lifetime of being tenderized, not just by life's challenges, but by its beauty too. Barrett has added fuel to my already flying jet, and he has taken me to places on the global map, and within myself that I would have never gone on my own. We are mutually supportive, loving, and guiding of one another's gifts. He sharpens my blade and I temper his—we are balanced. So it is with great joy that I share this endeavour with him and in doing so, I pray that other men will read this book and be changed by his example, that young women can use this book as a roadmap, and that the rest of us can tell our stories in a way that inspires not only others, but ourselves as well.

Every woman in this book has touched my life personally, and I am a better person for it. The time period during which each came into my life varies, but the impact does not. I am honored that they would let us share their stories, for I am keenly aware of the amount of trust that entails. We all have our own stories, and a particular way in which we share them. I share my story as an homage to all the powerful women who have helped form the tapestry of my life—I am ever grateful for all of their inspiration, support, and love.

As I review my life, I see three very distinct archetypes that shine beyond the others: The Healer, The Teacher, and The Artist. Each of these archetypes was sculpted through a process not unlike that of water against stone. I have placed the women interviewed here within one of these three archetypes, although likely they could have been placed in all three. These archetypes are neither female nor male, they are, however, needed now more than ever. They are the bridges in times of great transformation.

I was born into liminal space, literally between worlds, to a mother who thought she was giving birth to twins, but it was only me. Liminal means from neither here nor there, an in-between place, and in that space between things, there's a certain clarity that can be born. Perhaps it's because you don't belong there or anywhere, and are therefore not fixed or attached to any one place or story. My family happens to be Mexican American, though it always felt as if we were neither Mexican nor American. My liminal world was not only a physical place on a political border, it was a cultural and emotional place as well.

The Space Between Teacher And Student

Mama stayed at home with us kids, and dad was a teacher, but looking back I think he may have been a *Cuarandero*, a shaman of sorts. He always seemed mysterious and quiet, yet he was the person everyone went to for advice. He taught me how to navigate the space between worlds, through dreams, and then he helped me reconcile the thin line between dreams and waking reality. One of my earliest memories is of my father instructing me to teach Mexicans how to pronounce *American* like an American-born citizen, so that they might cross the border into the US without being stopped by immigration. Looking back, I see how radical that really was, but at the time, it was merely about giving families the opportunity to be together.

Because my father was a teacher, we all shared the same holidays, so we'd pile into the car and hit the road. The García girls would sing out loud with our favorite Mexican singers, as we drove off into the horizon. Mama loved Chente, Vicente Fernandez, and though my sister and I preferred Juan Gabriel and Ana Gabriel, we had no problem chiming in as Mama sang from the front seat. The mounting enthusiasm inevitably culminated into the release of one of my mother's famous *gritos*, a sort of impassioned shout or exclamation. We traveled all over Texas, Oklahoma, Kansas, Arkansas, and south into Mexico—anywhere we had *familia*. We had a lot of family too, because my father was one of 15 children, including two who were adopted, like my uncle Julio, who was exactly my father's age, so they grew up like twins. Julio died before I was born, and it is said that my dad was never quite the same after Julio's death.

As a child I would play in the streets, and without fail, someone would yell, "La Migra! La Migra! Run!" and we did. Immigration officers (La Migra) often patrolled our block, and we'd all run and hide, afraid that they would take us away, despite the fact that we were all citizens, born in the United States. Although it was a game, there was a fear—a deeper knowledge of being different, and it expressed itself through stories of what La Migra would do to us Mexicanos if we were caught.

I could see the Rio Grande from my bedroom window, and as I grew up, the militarization of the border grew up with me. It went from having no fence at all, to being chain link, to barbed wire, to a full steel wall. Machine gun posts were set up every mile or so, as were more and more armed patrol vehicles. It was a slow progression, and we were right in it, like frogs in slow boiling water, but somehow the violence of it was normalized and the obvious changes were too.

I used to love our trips to Mexico, and on one such visit, I began to notice that my sister's darker features and beauty were preferred in the northern part of Mexico, whereas further south, my fairer features were preferred. I remember what that felt like, and although I tried to understand the irrationality of it, the only thing I could come up with was that people liked what most resembled themselves. No matter how you cut it, it was made very clear that we were not Mexican, so ironically, I never felt more American than I did during our Mexican vacations. These early experiences led to my fascination with identity as a medley of characteristics by which we define ourselves, which are derived mainly from how others perceive us, what they expect from us, and a deep, innate, longing to be loved.

I went to public schools and I was an undiagnosed dyslexic—back in the 1970s, they didn't really diagnose or help people with dyslexia. When I reached 3rd grade, I was put into a remedial reading class and I felt very ashamed. I remember understanding that the letters in the words somehow flipped on me, so if the word I saw didn't make sense, it was probably because my brain was flipping the letters around. I started memorizing words in the dictionary, so that my mind could guess the word based on where it was in context of the sentence, and that's how I began to make up for my dyslexic deficiency.

I credit my cousin, Debbie, for giving me the gift of love for languages. She was constantly expanding my use of the words I had memorized, while at the same time constantly correcting my pronunciation, doing away with my Spanish accent altogether. This is how my identity around intellect was galvanized, and it was the place from where many of my future decisions would be made.

During my sophomore year of high school, my father left my mother, which made for a very unhappy home life. It lit a fire in me to ensure that I would never be as reliant on another person as my mother had been on my father. By the time I was 17, I was accepted to a college in Boston, which was the furthest place I could think of from El Paso, Texas. I flew to Boston to attend Northeastern University, not knowing anyone, or anything about Boston. I was there for a year and a half before my scholarship ran out, but since I had no way of paying for additional school, I moved to Iowa, where I had been offered a full-ride scholarship right out of high school. Unfortunately, that scholarship was no longer available, but I didn't care—Iowa was my Plan B. It was a very strange place, and I met the best and worst kind of people there.

I moved to Iowa with my eye on gaining residency, so that I would be eligible for in-state tuition at the University of Iowa. I was going to night school, working three jobs, and I lived off campus with a woman who ended up being mentally ill. She became increasingly paranoid, abusive, and even racist as things worsened. I just worked longer and longer hours, doing everything I could to stay away from the house and her. On one particular day, she verbally threatened me and made her point emphatically clear when she threw a piece of furniture at me. I ran off to work, narrowly escaping her abuse, but not without a high level of distress.

One of my jobs was at a Weight Watchers center, and one of the clients I had befriended was a doctor. He happened to be scheduled for a visit that day and he simply asked how I was doing, but that's all it took for my carefully hidden tears to rush forth. I decided on the spot that I had to let someone know what was going on, so why not him? That night, he and his wife drove me to the house and helped me gather all of my belongings, while my landlady/housemate yelled and screamed at us all. Her ranting continued to escalate the closer we got to completing our task, and I think it really traumatized the people who were so kindly standing by my side. Something about that experience felt incomplete until I spoke to the housing officials and made certain that she could never rent to another person again.

That same night, the doctor and his wife found a Reverend and his family to take me in for the night. I vividly remember sitting there having dinner with the family. Their four children were about my age, perhaps a little older, and they were all going out that night. They considerately asked if I'd like to join them—I was hesitant, but I went along anyway. All I can remember was looking at them with longing, a longing for that levity that comes with youth, and I was keenly aware of the fact that such innocence was not mine, nor would it ever be mine.

After that night, I didn't have any other place to go and I didn't have the heart to tell anyone. I became homeless for a time, and I slept under a bridge on campus for just over a week. There, I met a man who had been a professor at the university, but he had become such a ruined alcoholic that he lost everything—his professorship, his family, and his home. Alcoholism ran in my family too, so I was acutely aware of the nightmares that came with it, but I had never met someone so totally broken by the addiction. Still, he showed me where I'd be safest and how to navigate the situation. After a week under the bridge, I finally got a big enough paycheck that I went to the hotel on the university grounds to get a room. I found out that I could actually stay there and the cost would simply be added to my tuition bill, which was especially perfect given my situation.

During my stay in the campus hotel, I ended up in the hospital twice: once for a broken foot, and again when I had a very bad allergic reaction to a plant in my botany class. I didn't know anyone at all, so I just took care of myself. I remember calling my mother every Sunday and acting as if everything was OK, while secretly wishing I could just ask her to come and get me.

All total, I was under that bridge for 8 days and nights, and then I spent a month in the campus hotel before I saved up enough money to get an apartment. It wasn't a great apartment, and the building was basically in the projects, so it wasn't close to work or school, which meant that I had to take two buses to get anywhere. But at least I had a home.

I remember waiting for the bus every day and trying to connect with people, but most were very distant. They were all White, but I was too young to think that I was perceived as being that much different from them. Then one day, I woke up to the sound of fire trucks and a lot of commotion. I opened my front door and saw a burning cross. Again, I was too naive to think that it had anything to do with me, and it wasn't until a neighbor came over to see if I was OK that the reality became clear. She explained that it was the local KKK showing hatred towards me, "It was a warning," she said. I never would have thought the KKK would attack me, but I wasn't about to be made homeless again, and I wasn't about to be run out of my home, so I stuck it out. I never did find out exactly who did it, nor did they ever bother me again.

I feel the need to put this in perspective, as this was the Iowa KKK in 1990. Back then, I thought the KKK was a thing of the past, but now I fear it's only gotten worse in 2020. The fact that they would prey on a young Mexican woman who was simply trying to make her way through college shows how cowardly these men can be.

During the time I was writing this introduction, there was a news story about a White woman in Iowa who ran over a young Mexican girl because the girl "looked Mexican." As horrible as it is, it's fascinating to me that there can be these vortexes where everything and nothing has changed—hate is something I'll just never understand.

Those years experiencing a general lack of safety taught me how to live in the moment, how to be self-reliant, and most importantly, how to forgive. I began to notice that as soon as my mind grasped on to something for safety, that thing would shift. One can look at this statement and feel terrified, but in all honesty, it had the exact opposite effect on me. The truth of all things, is that the only constant is change. By understanding this fact deeply, I was able to transform the hatred that came towards me, and to overcome the parts of me that feared it. In that constant flux, I found infinite potential.

I was still enrolled at the University of Iowa, when my sister asked me to come home to help with my mother. I made my way back to El Paso, and to be honest, I felt like a total failure because I had no intention of ever going back to El Paso. However, the choice proved to be one of the best I ever made. There are a few reasons why the return was a good one, one being that I was already a psychology major, and the psychology department at the University of Texas at El Paso (UTEP) had just hired a whole new crew of Ph.D.s. They were excited about being there and doing new research, so I fell in with them immediately, it was perfect timing. They gave me every opportunity to excel, and I took every opportunity they offered me. I spent days and nights working in the labs and before I knew it, I was getting paid for doing what I loved to do. I was gaining all the experiences that would be necessary for a graduate school application: summer jobs, scholarships, publications, etc.

I also got permission as an undergraduate to take a graduate seminar on eyewitness memory and police lineup procedures. In the middle of the semester, my cousin was car-jacked and shot five times in the back as he was trying to run away, and I was the only witness—I had answered the door when the shooter arrived. I was able to work through the horror of sitting at home, afraid that the shooter would come back for me, coupled with the pressure the police had put on me for refusing to choose anyone from their line up, despite the fact that none of them matched my memory. I made that experience my project for the course, and I was able to test the lineup that had been shown to me, and thus prove that my already foggy memory of the perpetrator had been mishandled. I eventually joined that same professor in training the local police department on how to protect a witness's memory, and the best way to conduct an eyewitness lineup.

I started hanging out with graduate students too, because I was working in the labs so much, and that's how I knew that I wanted to go to graduate school in psychology. I took the Graduate Entrance Exam (GRE) and I totally bombed it! I didn't have the money to take a prep course, nor to take the test again, but I had, by that point, accumulated so much research experience, that I held firm to the belief that if a school couldn't look beyond my low GRE scores, then I didn't want to go to that school anyway. My professors thought I was crazy, and they chided me for being stubborn. They made it clear that they expected every single school to turn me down.

One of the places I applied was Tufts University, back in Boston, mainly because one of my undergraduate professors was applying for a job there too. We thought that it might be nice to continue working together, and although he didn't take the job, there was one man at Tufts who noticed my application and took the time to look further into my file. I had been accepted into a few graduate programs, but Tufts was offering me everything I wanted. I didn't miss the fact that the professor who advocated for me and became my mentor, was also named Julio García, just like my father's twin who had died so many years earlier. Julio was a Stanford alum, and he continued to work with his advisors, Claude Steele and Hazel Markus, both of whom became very influential in my own graduate work. Claude's work in particular was of interest to me, as it was driven by the civil rights movement and his interest in the psychological implications of race riots.

My experience at Tufts was very challenging from the outset, especially when I came to the realization that none of the other professors wanted me there, and that Julio had really fought for me to get in. I hit the ground running and was well into my master's project before the first fall semester had even begun. A jealous graduate student went into my advisor's office, stole my personal file, and therein saw my low GRE scores. She proceeded to share it's contents with several other graduate students, and then she started a bet as to when I would flunk out.

At the end of my second semester, one of the older students, whom I had befriended, told me all about it. I went up to the girl who stole my file, put a $100 bill in front of her and said, "Four years and I'll have my Ph.D." She looked at me puzzled, so I added, "Well, you're betting as to when I'll flunk out, aren't you?" She began to cry and tremble as I continued, "In four years, I will finish this program with a Ph.D. to my name." And so I did—I finished in four years at only 27 years of age, faster than even *la chica de apuestas* (the betting girl) herself. More importantly, I finished knowing my worth as a woman and a Latina. I wasn't about to go around feeling like an imposter in my own life. This process was hard enough, and it meant not letting someone who didn't even know me put a value on me. It's important to confront certain people head-on like that, because you just might be protecting some other person from the same plight in the future.

The Line Between Artist And Revolutionary

During my third year, a fellow graduate student who really loved to dance, called me up one day to tell me that a Tango master, known only as the Black Panther, was giving a seminar at Harvard. It was only a couple of train stops from Tufts, and although I didn't have enough money for the whole week seminar, I decided to register for a half-day class. I remember the first moment I saw the Tango master walk in, because he had this beautiful long black hair, and as he entered, he reached out to take a stick from the corner of the room. The music was cued up and he began to dance with the stick, and before my very eyes, that stick became the most beautiful woman I'd ever seen. From that moment on, I knew that if I surrendered to him, he had the ability to make me look as beautiful as he had that stick.

It's comical to say this out loud, but I swear it's the truth. Up to that point in my life, I was considered the least gifted dancer in my family. I was too rigid, "Suelta las caderas!" they would say, which means loosen those hips, adding that I was thinking too much—and they were right. I learned to surrender to the dance and to the Tango master, and he indeed transformed me in the process. He gave me the rest of the seminar for free, and then later asked if I would step in for his partner, who had suffered an injury. That was my big experience in professional Tango dancing, and I even got to compete in Buenos Aires, the original city where the Tango was born.

I had also studied martial arts in Boston, back when I was an undergraduate, and well before my "Tango career." I studied Shotokan Karate to be exact, and since I had seen a Karate master in action, I was able to recognize the same mastery in the Tango dancer.

There's a deep parallel between dancing and martial arts, and there is also something very spiritual and mystical about the art of movement itself. Moving through time and space, based on the architecture of body and sound, opened my eyes to something much deeper—it changed my relationship to myself, and the way I moved through the world. Needless to say, this theory of movement was a far cry from the *Cumbias* I grew up dancing to, but both required moving like liquid through a gravityless, velvet sky.

While at Tufts, I was also given the opportunity to co-teach *The History Of American Sports* with one of Tufts most beloved professors, Dr. Gerald Gill. I had been given a teaching scholarship, whereby I could pick a teaching mentor and then teach a course with them. When I asked Dr. Gill if he would be my mentor, he responded by asking, "Now, why would a psychologist ever want to teach a history course?" My response was that he, as an African American, had created a space where people of color, and all people really, could be safe and thrive. I wanted to be like him, I said. "Well Lisette, this won't be easy. There are ten books that I would require you to read and comprehend well enough to teach, before we even set foot in the classroom. Are you willing to do that?" I said yes, and proceeded to work my butt off for the next four months. Teaching *The History Of American Sports* with Dr. Gill was one of the greatest experiences of my life. He moved me deeply and I loved him as a mentor and also as a friend. Years later, he would die alone in his chair at home, a fact that still haunts me to this day.

Right about the same time as I was preparing to teach with Dr. Gill, I met the late, great Dr. Badi Foster. Badi was also a professor at Tufts, and he was the head of the Lincoln Filene Center for Citizenship and Public Affairs. He was teaching a course on leadership, and I somehow convinced my advisor that it would fit within my needed coursework. It was an inspiring course, and it really opened my mind to many of the ways different people around the world were dedicating their lives to public service. I remember meeting the President of UNESCO and wishing so instensely that I could be like him.

When Badi was hired as president of the Phelps Stokes Fund (PSF) in 2000, he hired me before I had even defended my dissertation. My advisors were not happy that I did not go straight into academia, but I never once regretted my decision. I moved the defense of my dissertation up by five months just to take the job at PSF, and that meant I was literally working 24/7 for five months, just to get it done in time to start my new job. The short title of my dissertation was, "Protection and Assertion of Cultural Identity," which looked at collectivistic versus individualistic cultures. I showed how even one's most mundane choices reflect who we think we are in any given context, and what we do to defend that identity.

After completion of my dissertation and its successful defense, all of it within that four-year period that people had betted against, I spent one transformative year working at Badi's side. I had moved to Washington D.C., where the main office of the Phelps Stokes Fund were located, but I traveled almost the entire time. I attended meetings with Badi, where the old civil rights leaders would gather. They understood that the fight for civil rights was an ongoing one, and that experience brought my own life into perspective because indeed, the battle for civil rights is still being fought today. I can still remember walking into the room and feeling completely inadequate amongst some of the most important people of our time. The air seemed thicker, and there was a gravitas to every word that was spoken. At the table sat the likes of Coretta Scott King and Maya Angelou, and I sat in the corner taking notes furiously, feeling very much like a fly on the wall. Then one day Maya turned to me and asked, "And what do you think about that, little brown sister?" I don't remember what she was referring to, I only remember what it felt like when our eyes met, and in doing so, she empowered me to take my seat at the table.

In fact, it was during that very same period of time that I met and became great friends with the musician, Lenny Kravitz. It turned out that Lenny knew Maya Angelou very well, because of his mother Roxy, and in fact, Lenny used Maya's bus to tour in. I was physically at the center of this elite fellowship of African American leaders, and somehow, I found myself working amongst them, trying my hardest to absorb every last bit of the mojo that dripped from those powerful people.

I learned to be fully in myself, to be beautiful, strong, kind, smart, passionate, and to be really proud of being Mexican—of being *Poderosa*. I learned to be these things all at once, and not to diminish any one for the other. For example, I used to try to downplay my looks because I wanted to be seen as smart, and I thought if I were too passionate, I would be perceived as being emotional and weak. After those experiences, I strived to be fully me, and I have kept those beautiful women of power in my heart and as my guides from that time onward. I am equally grateful to Dr. Gill, Dr. Foster, and Lenny for letting a young Mexican woman shine. The world needs more men like them.

During my time at the Phelps Stokes Fund, I worked to improve enrollment at historically black colleges through a Single Mothers program. It was meant to support these women by providing housing for both the mother and her baby, so that young mothers could finish their bachelor degrees. The program was already in place at Texas College, and my part was to help recruit Latina's into the program as well. I even did some work in West Africa helping to train former child combatants, who were returning from a horrific civil war, as they tried to reintegrate into their culture. The majority of my work, however, was to help facilitate programs that focused on bridging the divide between Latinos and African Americans.

I was 29 years old when the September 11th attack happened at the World Trade Center. As a result, the federal government withdrew much of the funding for the Phelps Stokes Fund, and we were eventually let go from our positions. Luckily, upon moving to New York City, I was offered a teaching position at John Jay College of Criminal Justice. I had always maintained a line of research in the eyewitness realm, and walking down the hall at John Jay on that very first day, I passed a door that had a name on a placard: Steven Penrod. I knew that name from my early days in the law and psychology field, and I couldn't believe that it would be the same person—but it was.

Steven had just taken a job there too, so I fell right in and within days I was working in his lab. Not long after that, I was leading the lab as a Postdoctoral Fellow and had the possibility of a tenure-track position, but that comes with its own story—and a caveat.

In the years that I was at John Jay, it went from being an NYPD training hub, to being one of the country's preeminent forensic science programs. This particular period of time also coincided with the American obsession with forensic TV programs like *CSI: Crime Scene*

Investigation, much to our chagrin. However, I loved the diversity of the student body, and teaching a class in Spanish was a bit of a trick I used to help English speakers think about how hard it is for students whose first language is not English. It was really quite enjoyable, and I had the opportunity to teach all of my favorite courses. I was simultaneously leading one of the largest research labs in the psychology department, and I was able to recreate the love and vigor for research that I had experienced as both an undergraduate and graduate student, just a few years earlier. We worked hard, but we also had a great deal of fun, and all of this was happening in tandem with my intensifying Buddhist studies.

I had applied for a tenure track position my first year at John Jay, but I was neither focused enough, nor was I ready to jump into academia full time, so I wasn't offered a position. A few years later, however, there were more positions open in the psychology department, and this time I was ready. I had proven myself as a teacher and a researcher, but despite my obvious fit, I was told that I should not apply for the position. I think their exact words were, "Lisette, you don't interview well. Maybe just sit this one out." I took that as an indication that I wouldn't be seriously considered for a tenure track position, and I was pretty upset about it. In hindsight, I see that this was one of those monumental events when the direction of one's life can change forever.

My Buddhist studies had been deepening for years, and it was culminating in the opportunity to do a three-year, three-month, three-day silent meditation retreat in the southern desert of Arizona. When the department didn't give me the opportunity to apply for a tenure track position, I put my mind towards participating in the meditation retreat instead, and to leave academia all together. Then, as it always happens, my resolve was tested once again.

In June of 2004, months after all the hires had been made in the psychology department, I got a visit from the head of the department and the only African American professor in the department. "Congratulations! We were just given some extra money for a minority hire and we want it to be you!" I must admit that I was thrilled at first, it was what I had been working towards for a very long time, and I accepted the position on the spot without a thought. But I had a nagging feeling that there was something really screwed up about the way the offer was made. That is to say, I was offered the job simply because I was a minority, and they were very clear in telling me not to go around "waving my Mexican flag." It was not because of all the great research and teaching I had done. A week later I was at a faculty meeting, and as I looked at all the faces around the table, my whole life fell into perspective. "That will be you in 30 years—is this what you want?" my inner voice asked. I realized that I simply wanted more out of life, I wanted to delve into the true inner workings of the mind, and thus, I resigned from my newly appointed tenure-track position.

All of this was happening in New York City, one of the most diverse cities in the world, yet my race was still clipping me at the knees. The fact that my department was betting on me taking a "minority position" showed the systemic racism that is inherent in academia, even though they couldn't see it for themselves. To be fair, the African American professor who was present when I was offered the position, later apologized. He said that it had taken him some time to put himself in my position, but that he understood just how awful that must have felt. I always appreciated that he did that, but this was not my first brush with systemic racism, and strangely, because I eventually left the academic system altogether, it would be one of my last—for a time.

Three weeks later, Steven Penrod and I were informed that we had been awarded a very large research grant in an amount over $300,000. For the following three years, I no longer had to teach, but I did get to keep my research lab, continue my research, and I was able to pay my students well. During that time, I also began to travel back and forth to Arizona in preparation for my upcoming three-year silent meditation retreat. What had once seemed like the most important thing in the world—to become a university professor, was now a distant second to my spiritual enlightenment. I was about to take the deep dive into the realm of mind in search of God.

The Line Between Meditator And Healer

Being Mexican American, I was raised as a traditional Catholic, and as a child I had a very strong faith. For example, at the age of five, I made an internal agreement with the Virgen de Guadalupe that if she blessed my grandmother and improved her health, then I would go to her cathedral in Mexico City and make my way to her altar on my knees. When we got to Mexico City, there was so much traffic that my father wanted to skip the cathedral altogether. At that moment, I began to cry passionately, saying nothing of my secret deal with La Virgen, and only that we must go to the cathedral at all costs. My father dropped me and my mother off at the cathedral, and I was given the opportunity to complete my pilgrimage—and my oath to La Virgen.

Fast-forward 30 years, and I'm in New York City where I attended a talk by a Tibetan Buddhist monk, who had just returned from completing a three-year silent retreat. Needless to say, what he had done fascinated me, and what he shared in that talk excited both my spiritual and intellectual sides. The main premise of his talk was about how reality isn't an objective thing "out there," but rather that our minds are like movie projectors, and we each create our own realities based on how we've treated others in the past. This is the law of *Karma*.

I heard a few people talking about a famous Tibetan Buddhist *Lama* (teacher) named Khen Rinpoche, who had fled Tibet during the Chinese invasion in 1950. He had made his way to India and was told, by the Dalai Lama himself, to continue on to the United States to serve at a temple in New Jersey. Khen Rinpoche was about to begin a series of teachings, and everyone was about to pile into a car to attend. I felt this incredible urgency to join them—and so I did.

At this point in my life, I had accomplished everything I had ever set my mind to do, yet there was still something missing. I looked at my academic colleagues and I saw sadness and misery, and although I wasn't necessarily sad myself, I felt as if I was looking at my own future. The practice of Buddhism and this new worldview excited me, and I knew that I needed to investigate it further. As a psychologist, I was drawn to explore the depths of the mind and heart from a totally different perspective. I was now ready to enter the world of Spirit.

The time going back and forth between New York and Arizona in preparation for my own three-year retreat was a rigorous and intense period. Why does a person do a retreat of that kind in the first place, you may ask? I can only speak for myself, but I needed to answer these specific questions:

Does the ancient wisdom of Buddhism, with its mechanisms for the practice of meditation, overcome the limits of the mind? Does this practice still work in this modern day and age? Do these teachings, which were meant for men, also work for women? If so, how could the radical choice I was making as a woman, and the wisdom gained due to those choices, be distilled into teachings for others who might not want to be as radical as I was?

Even my research began to reflect my deepening Buddhist practice. I had an opportunity to go to India to work with Dr. Kiran Bedi in New Delhi, who was the first woman to join the Indian Police Service. She remained in the service for 35 years, before taking voluntary retirement in 2007 as the Director General of Bureau Police Research and Development. She was an activist and a trailblazer, and she was best known for transforming one of India's most notorious prisons. More importantly, she herself transcended innumerable obstacles, including every 'ism in the book. She represented to me, as she did for many other women, an incredible force of will, and thus, was a perfect role model.

In 1993, she became the Inspector General of Delhi Prisons and she implemented several reforms that won her global acclaim. The most radical of these reforms was introducing meditation to the inmates, allowing an area to be designated for their practice. She also allotted time for Vipassana meditation retreats within the prison, which resulted in lower criminal recidivism, less waste, fewer visits to the doctor, and fewer incidences of violence. My plan was to study this method and quantify it in such a way that I could pitch meditation to American prisons and try to implement some of Dr. Bedi's reforms.

Unfortunately, the US prison system is built upon a corrupt foundation of corporate extraction that values money over people, and it uses punitive methods on the prisoners, rather than real and lasting reform for the incarcerated. As you would expect, my progressive ideas fell upon the deaf ears of those who were only motivated by profit and greed.

My last year out in the world before the beginning of my three-year retreat was like preparing for my own death, which in a way, it was. I said all my good-byes to my family and friends, I mended whatever hurt feelings needed attention, I closed all my bank accounts, paid off everything, and gave the rest away. In doing so, all of the Buddhist practices I had done up to that point began to ripen, and I had very strong experiential insights into the nature of reality. My conceptual mind had begun to fracture (a good thing), and during this period I remember that I couldn't even keep a screw tightened. It was so obvious and funny how, quite literally, everything in my life was coming undone.

I was in perpetual bliss, a power and beauty that comes from being completely openhearted, and by the time the retreat began, my mind was already deeply into it. Part of me thought that in saying my goodbyes I was leaving the world behind, when in truth, I brought the whole world with me. As it turns out, we were never separate.

There are far too many details about those three years in silent retreat, which I cannot share here simply for brevity's sake. That is a different book entirely—perhaps my next one. That being said, a retreat is like your life: it never goes exactly as you envision it, and how could one even begin to imagine the depths of the mind? I intended to explore the place beyond ego and identity, and the only way to do that is to break one's conceptual mind. In doing so, all kinds of things are upended, and revealed.

A three-year, silent meditation retreat is like walking on the blade of a sword—it can free you, or it can kill you. My day-to-day existence went like this: I would wake up at 2 am and meditate until 6:30 am, then I would say my mantras, and by 8 am I was meditating again. I would meditate until 12 noon, and then I would go outside to breathe in some fresh air. The sweet fragrance of creosote, *Larrea Tridentata*, a high desert shrub, wafting through the air after a spring shower is still one of my favorite things in this world.

I always carried cashews in my pockets, and all the animals would swing by for a treat. The squirrel would stick his paw into my pocket and sit next to me as he ate. The fox would come by and check things out, and at first I had to place a cashew a couple of feet away, which he would grab and run. Then, after a month or so, he would take the nut from my hand and eat it there next to me. Have you ever watched a fox eat? Half the food falls out of the sides of their very small mouths and they never pick up what has fallen on the ground! He reminded me of the Cookie Monster.

By 1 pm, I would begin my yoga practice and I would usually do a very nice, slow two-hour practice. At 3 pm, I would drink a smoothie, and by 5 pm I was back on the meditation cushion. At 7 pm, I would have a very light dinner, which was usually just some veggies and rice. Food was dropped off every two weeks, and I learned very quickly that some vegetables spoiled much faster than others, so broccoli, Brussels sprouts, and kale became the staples. I would then finish off my day with a light gratitude meditation.

I had spent a lot of time scouring my mind before retreat, for any affliction that might come back to haunt me. Every teacher that I had spoken with said that I would have to face all of my greatest fears. It was true.

I learned that I had a deep fear of going blind, so I began to walk around in the vast desert alone on dark moon nights. I could hardly see my hand in front of my face, and I had to learn to see with my feet, taking slow and deliberate steps on the uneven earth. The big and unexpected fear that came up had to do with not being loved, and I saw how much that fear had driven even the most basic decisions that I'd made throughout my life. In fact, I came to understand that the need for love was the foundation upon which all other aspects of my identity stood—the need to be smart, the need to be of service to the world, and even the desire to be kind.

This realization came most strongly during the second year of the retreat when I literally felt the world forget about me. That pull of even my own mother's mind was gone. This was interesting to me as a psychologist, because one's very identity, one's whole existence, is so strongly reliant on others and what they think of you. When that was gone, I simply began to dissolve. I became like the tree in the forest that fell and there is no one around to hear it, the great question or *koan* being, "Does it make a sound?" I went outside and laid on the sandy desert ground, feeling the pieces of me fall away, and when I opened my eyes, I realized that my fox friend had brought his whole family, and all five of them had taken their places around me, floating with me in the realm of no-self.

It was soon after that when my conceptual mind, which had previously held that time and space were fixed things, began to see its mistake. I found that all the ancient teachings were indeed valid, that women are just as open to those realizations as men, and that all of the stories of the lineage holders that seemed so fantastical, indeed, impossible fairy tales, were not only possible, but also highly probable. The barriers around my heart broke open, and I learned how to love without needing to be loved back.

The most difficult part of the whole retreat experience, however, was its ending. I had to rebuild my life, learn to speak again, and sew together a notion of self in order to function in the world. I eventually made my way back to New York City, and it wasn't long after that when a dear friend of mine was diagnosed with a particularly rare form of cancer. Her twin daughters were 10-years-old at the time, so I dedicated my life to taking care of them for three years, until she was healthy enough to be a full-time mother again. I saw those three years as the gift that gave me my second wing. One wing was from the three-year retreat, which gave me the wing of wisdom, and the three years of service to my friend and her children gave me the wing of love and compassion. That family became my family, and we helped each other through exceedingly difficult circumstances, and as a result, we loved each other even more.

When I met my husband, Barrett Martin, through a mutual friend, the timing was perfect. My friend was cancer-free and rebuilding her own life with her family, and I was headed to Thailand to gather the experience in support of a form of healing I had developed in the retreat. Meanwhile, Barrett was headed to Wales in the UK to produce a Welsh rock band. Barrett was unlike any man I had ever met. He was confident yet humble, wise and intelligent in every sense of the word, but best of all he had done *the work*. Here, I am referring to that deep spiritual work that grounds you when everyone else is being rocked by a topsy-turvy world. I moved to the Pacific Northwest to be with him and we began the next chapter of our lives together, traveling the world and riding the balance between love and wisdom, growth and kindness.

Not long after moving to Seattle, my sister and I began a small business conducting hardship evaluations for immigrants who want to keep their families together during, and beyond, the arduous process of legal immigration. The stories I hear everyday remind me of how fortunate I am as a person, and because I am part of the struggle for immigrant's basic liberties, I feel empowered in a way that is strikingly similar to how I felt at age three, when my father had me teaching Mexican's how to say *American* like an American. I get to defend those who come to this country and have become a vital part of the fabric of the United States of America. Looking back on my life, I see all that I overcame was merely to ready me to serve the world and it's people in this particular way, and I'm grateful to have a partner in life with whom to do that work.

As I wrote this story, I gazed out of my office window in Washington State and realized that I was looking at Vancouver Island in British Columbia, Canada, with only the Strait of Juan de Fuca separating us. It is yet another liminal space, a place between worlds. My life has always been about breaking down borders—I've faced them down my entire life, whether it was the Texas-Mexico border, the American-Canadian border, a racial border, a gender border, or even a spiritual border. I understand that most people are imprisoned because of the boundaries they hold up as being real, and there is a part of me that loves to show them otherwise.

We are so much more powerful than any of the divisions we see in the world, that's why this book is important, and that's why Barrett's participation is a vital piece of this project. It is, in essence, a form of revolt against the duality of masculine versus feminine wisdom.

All of the women in this book have overcome something enormous, and always it was because they found the power to do so within themselves. These women are all Poderosas—extraordinary, ordinary Mighty Ones. They are sublime examples of the three very distinct archetypes, which shape our world: The Healer, The Teacher, and The Artist. We are all an essential piece of the puzzle of life, and like the women in this book, we have all been sculpted by a power that is beyond good or bad.

Each of us shines in our own way, and likely more than one, and that is because, we are all mighty.

THE HEALERS

PODEROSAS

Dr. Angie Chavez

Pediatric Intensivist & Cancer Survivor

"A person cannot be a good physician if they have never been sick themselves."

-Doctor's Proverb

Lisette: I met Angie Chavez while attending junior high school in El Paso, Texas, and I can't recall if we had a class together or not, but certainly our friends overlapped. One friend that we did not have in common was my dear friend Renee. She and I were in the same troupe of Brownies and later, Girl Scouts. Renee and her beautiful parents lived in their elegant home just around the block from our infinitely more modest home. I remember being 7-years-old and feeling a bit envious, especially when my life had been turned upside down as a result of my brother's car accident and the ensuing efforts to rehabilitate him. I looked at Renee and her carefree family, wishing that I was her, and that her family was mine.

Then Renee got sick, she lost her hair, and then she passed away. I was told she had leukemia, but I had no idea what that meant. When she lost her hair and courageously came to our Girl Scout meetings, my envy turned to love—I loved her beautiful smile, and her kind and playful way of moving through the world. I remember asking her how

41

it was all going, and she responded with softness in her eyes that she wasn't sure she could make it. All I could think to do was hug her. After Renee passed away, her beautiful home fell into ruins and her parents eventually divorced, because the hole she had left was too much for them to bear. It was only then that I understood the horror of cancer.

When Angie Chavez was diagnosed with cancer, I recognized the same courage and beauty that I saw in my friend Renee. I understood the gravity of her situation when it was explained to me, and I understood what it took for Angie to show up for the world in the way that she did, each and every day.

There is an innocence that is lost in sickness and death, and in Mexican culture it isn't hidden away from children, although it might be downplayed while the adults figure out how they feel, which can vary from moment to moment. The philosopher Emilio Uranga stated that, "To be Mexican is to suffer from a peculiar kind of madness, a state of being characterized by a violent oscillation between optimism and pessimism." That is to say, to be Mexican is to sway intensely back and forth, between grasping and aversion—although I'd argue that it is a human condition. It is a particular kind of madness, and it is nowhere more evident than in our attitude towards sickness, death, and our relationship to them. I share this not because I hold this particular worldview, or this malady as it were, but because it is what we were brought up around. It is all at once magical and cynical, it can save people, and it can also imprison them.

Part of me always knew that Angie would make it, she had a fight in her that Renee was never given a chance to develop. I remember when we were applying to universities, I was so grateful that not only had Angie been accepted at her top choices, but that she would get the opportunity to finally live her life, not as a cancer survivor, but as a woman. To my recollection, Angie had always wanted to become a doctor, and I had no doubt that that was exactly what she would become. She was smart, kind, and purposeful back then, just as she is now, and it was an honor when she agreed to have this conversation over dinner at a barbeque near the hospital where she works in El Paso.

Angie, please tell us about your early childhood—what was it like growing up as a Mexican-American girl in El Paso, Texas? And how old were you when you got sick?

Angie: I grew up in a very traditional Mexican family. Dad was the provider and patriarch, and mom was there to nurture and take care of us kids. We just went to school like everybody else. Looking back, I realize that we grew up poor, but I didn't understand it at the time, because I was generally pretty happy, and I had everything I needed. Then—and I don't remember exactly how this happened, but when I was about 14-years-old, I felt a mass in my lower abdomen. I thought it was just weight at first, but it was my mom who realized that I was actually getting sick, and I didn't even realize it. So I went to the doctor, and I was immediately diagnosed with cancer. My life changed in one second—one test result and my life changed forever. I didn't really understand what was going on, but I knew something was wrong because they admitted me to the hospital that same evening.

Lisette: You were so young Angie, were you scared, or what were your most obvious emotions?

Angie: I wasn't really scared, because I didn't understand what cancer was yet. I met my oncologist, and I had my first surgery that week. It turned out to be malignant ovarian cancer in my right ovary. I remember that it was late at night when the oncologist came to visit me after the surgery, and then I was discharged and the chemotherapy began right away. That's when I finally realized I had cancer, but my mom couldn't even utter the word cancer, so she minimized it by saying it was a small tumor, but it was of course much worse than that.

Lisette: What was it like getting chemo treatments at such a young age? That must have been very hard.

Angie: All the kids around me were sick and bald, and then I lost my hair too. It was incredibly traumatic to lose my hair, because I was on the freshman cheerleading squad and this all happened the summer before high school—that's when I started my chemo treatments. My life was suddenly all about going to the doctor. You know, your vanity is so important at that age, and I was a cheerleader! I thought, I can't go to school like this, I look like an alien, and I didn't even recognize myself. It was very hard to deal with.

Lisette: How did you make it through school, and were you able to keep cheerleading and stay on the squad?

Angie: I kept going to school, and my cheerleader girlfriends would come visit me at home. They would come over to the house, and they'd joke around and treat me like I wasn't sick. My best friend Mindy found me a wig—I was so embarrassed, but it was really a breakthrough. It helped me to make light of the situation. I remember that they made me come to a slumber party, and we were going out that night to a little teenybopper club called, "21 And Below." They found an outfit that fit me, they dressed me all up, and I wore my wig out in public for the first time. And then at the club, I was the only one who got asked to dance —in my new wig!

Barrett: Well that's awesome! I bet that helped your spirit a little?

Angie: I just wanted to be normal like everybody else. I didn't want to stand out or be in the spotlight, I just wanted to blend in. But that experience inspired me to go back to school with confidence, so the world wouldn't think I was dying of cancer.

Lisette: Did your doctors give you any kind of prognosis during your treatment?

Angie: I have no idea, because I was only 14-years-old at the time, so if they did, I don't remember. I do remember that when I started the chemo, I was crying and scared, and they had to change the chemical treatment because it wasn't working at first. I just remember that I cried a lot, and my mom had so much fear and worry.

Barrett: How did your dad deal with it?

Angie: My dad didn't participate at all. It was just my mom and I.

Lisette: Did the fact that you were so young—did that help in your recovery?

Angie: No it didn't, because unfortunately lots of kids die of cancer, so age doesn't really have that much to do with it. And chemo has many bad side effects. A while back, I had a conversation with a doctor at a cancer survivor's clinic, and I was told that I wouldn't be able to have children because of all the chemo I had as a young woman. The chemo drugs can even put you at risks for other blood disorders, like leukemia, for example.

Lisette: Wow, so the chemo they use to treat one kind of cancer, can actually cause the emergence of another type of cancer? That seems really counterintuitive, like the cure for one, is the poison for another.

Angie: Yes, and I'll give you another example on this. I was doing 120 hours a week as a resident doctor, and I became a pediatric fellow in the Intensive Care Unit at the University of Florida in Gainesville. It took me a total of 14 years to become an ICU doctor.

I was waiting to see this little boy, who was going to receive a kidney transplant from his father. As I was looking through his background, I saw that he had experienced renal failure from the same chemo drugs I had received. So these chemo drugs saved him from cancer, but they shut down and destroyed his kidneys. We were able to save him, but it was a real eye-opener about how dangerous chemo treatment can really be.

And then before the end of that three-year fellowship, there was another kid who came into the ICU who was very ill with heart failure. He needed a cardiac transplant, because his heart had failed as a result of chemo, and again, it was the same chemo drug that I had received. I am so grateful that this didn't happen to me, but I'm not special, I was just lucky. I remember being so sick, but by the grace of God, I did not succumb to some of those other diseases.

Lisette: You went through your chemotherapy about 30 years ago, are those drugs even still used today, or have they been eliminated?

Angie: Yes, they still use them! There is a certain threshold that they won't go over, but yes, those drugs are still being used today. It is a real risk, and I saw the truth of it later as a doctor myself.

Lisette: Let's go back a little, back to when you were still in high school, going through those chemo treatments—and still cheerleading!

Angie: Back in 1986 in El Paso, all I had was cheerleading for my escape. I would cry after my chemo treatments, go to sleep, and then get up and go to school. My doctors were really great though, and I made the sophomore cheerleading squad. My routine was pretty set every week: my mom took me to chemo on Friday, I'd miss school that day, but I would still make squad practice later that afternoon. I just kept grinding, and I just kept going, because I didn't know anything different than that. I think about social media today, and I'm so lucky that didn't exist back then.

Barrett: You're a warrior Angie, that's obvious just from sitting here with you. You kept your eyes on the prize.

Angie: Well, there were a few football games I just couldn't attend because the chemo was so bad, and I was too sick to make the game.

Lisette: Didn't you have to have surgery a second time? What was that situation?

Angie: Yes, my doctors thought the cancer had come back based on the new scans, so I had to have another operation, but that time it was just a benign cyst.

Lisette: How long was it until they gave you the all clear, that you were cancer-free?

Angie: I stopped going to the doctor at the end of my freshman year in college, so it was all through high school and into my first year of college. During those first two years of high school, I was bald and wearing a wig, and then later in my second year, I started growing my hair again. I was the bald cheerleader!

Lisette: That's so powerful Angie, because there was this love, and pride, and hope, and joy surrounding you.

Angie: I was really just trying to show up and be a normal teenager.

Lisette: Did you have any boyfriends, or boy crushes back then?

Angie: Yes, I did have a boyfriend! It just so happened that on Thursday nights, there was an evening group of chemo patients, and there was a young boy who had testicular cancer. His brother would sometimes come with him, and his brother became my first boyfriend.

Lisette: Did he take you to any of the dances?

Angie: Yes, he took me to his homecoming and the prom, but he was a couple years older than me, so he graduated earlier than I did. He didn't care about my wig at all, he was very much in love with me.

Lisette: That's beautiful.

Angie: Yeah, he was so young and he had such a good heart.

Lisette: Can we talk about how you went from being, as you said, the bald cheerleader, to being one of the first Pediatric Intensivists in El Paso?

Angie: Well, I applied to several colleges and I ended up going to Saint Mary's in San Antonio, because they were very interested in me and they offered me a great scholarship. I went off to college and that was probably the best time in my life. Those four years were just amazing, because I wasn't sick anymore. It was such freedom, because there is nothing better than your health. I was becoming a young adult, I was figuring out who I was, and it was a great time for personal discovery.

I was kind of smart, I was getting good grades, I met a lot of like-minded people, and I had a vision for my future. I healed in that environment because as a Christian, I didn't realize how broken and angry I was with God about everything I had experienced. Being there helped me to reconcile a lot of my anger and sadness. I didn't have all the answers, but I found peace and I got closer to God. I had some really good friends there too, and I met my first husband as well, when I was a freshman. He was already in the military, and we got married right after college.

Lisette: And then how did you pick your medical school?

Angie: I graduated Summa Cum Laude (highest honors) from Saint Mary's University, and I got accepted into the San Antonio Medical School. I did my residency there in general pediatrics, and then I moved to the University of Florida in Gainesville to do my ICU fellowship. Saint Mary's was truly a gift for me, I had a lot of fun there, I accomplished a huge amount, I fell in love, and I started my medical career. And I found a deep relationship with God—that's a lot of good things in four years!

Lisette: Well, I think you had some making up to do! Can you tell us why you chose pediatrics? Was it because you had that cancer experience as a young girl?

Angie: When I had that second surgery in high school, when they thought the cancer had come and back spread to my liver—that was a really terrible experience. It was a much bigger surgery than the first one, and it was done by a surgeon who was not a pediatric surgeon. He was just a regular, adult surgeon. Looking back at it now as a physician, I realize that the pediatric medicine in El Paso was really lacking at the time.

That surgeon gave me a 13" scar, and the recovery was really, really tough, even though they didn't find any more cancer. I felt so bad after that second surgery, it was worse than anything I had gone through up to that point, and I was still going through chemo treatments. I really thought I was going to die. They didn't have any of the anti-nausea drugs or anything to ease the suffering, so I was puking all the time after my chemo treatments, except now I had all of my abdominal muscles severed in the form of a 13" scar. I seriously thought I was going to die. I had to have real mental fortitude to get through that, and I think that's part of why I chose pediatrics, so I could help children avoid those kinds of doctors.

Lisette: Was the University of Florida known for its pediatrics department?

Angie: Well, I knew I had to leave Texas after medical school or I would never leave home. I also really needed the experience of another medical school, so I took the offer to go to Gainesville. And then a year after my ICU fellowship ended, I had another health scare. I felt another mass in my abdomen, but because I was now a doctor, my colleagues gave me really great treatment right away. The prognosis was that it could be ovarian cancer again, and if so, I was likely going to die. I started talking with my husband about end of life decisions and all that, and then I had the surgery. It turned out it was just another cyst and not cancerous, but the whole experience has taught me to be much more in touch with my mortality. This is why I hike in the mountains and run all the time. I can't say I'll be able to do that when I retire, because I know how fragile life is. I've run 20 half-marathons, and the first one I did was at the age of 38!

Barrett: Wow, that's amazing Angie! That's also why you are such a great doctor, because you understand what it's like to be really sick. That is the archetype of the great healer—the one who has been wounded deeply, is also the one with the greatest ability to heal others.

Angie: I think I have a unique perspective that other doctors don't necessarily have, but sometimes you have to put that away in order to function professionally. Because ultimately we are surgeons and ICU doctors, and patients expect that we have some kind of special knowledge or power that can save them. We have to have that confidence, and we can't get scared. Like when a teenager shows up in the ICU with cancer, I really have to have the courage to take charge of the situation and give them the best care.

Lisette: Do you ever tell them your personal story?

Angie: No, not really, because in the ICU, there's no time for that kind of thing. When they come in, I'm doing a lot of stuff quickly, making decisions on treatments and medications, to keep them from getting sicker or possibly dying. I don't really have time to tell them my story, and I don't think they'd really want to hear it anyway.

Lisette: What does that look like when they come into the ICU? A kid is sick, they are brought into the emergency room for diagnosis, and then they get sent up to you. How does that play out on your side?

Angie: OK, let's say they show up with an overwhelming, serious infection. They show up in the ER, they get diagnosed, and they are already calling us up in the ICU. Let's say the child needs a special procedure, so we start the central lines and medications, and it has to be done quickly, because children can die quickly. Intubation happens, labs, X-rays, scans, interpreting what they need, and applying it to the patient. It can all happen very fast, and they may be so sick that I have to be very careful, especially right after surgery when the potential for a crash is very close.

Lisette: How are you able to go home and unwind after all this, how do you leave your work and be normal again?

Angie: You kind of learn that during your training. So when I get home, I like to do the dishes and the normal mundane stuff, like sitting on the couch, when I just disconnect from everything. You have to protect yourself, because the next day you are doing it all over again. My husband can usually tell when I have had a bad day.

Lisette: Well, El Paso clearly needed a children's hospital, considering that the city has over half a million people. How did that whole process begin, because building a hospital is a major endeavor?

Angie: It had been in the works for over 20 years, and then all the pediatricians in El Paso went to Austin to convince the legislature that the city really needed a children's hospital. There were no specialists in El Paso, so if your kid was sick, you had to leave El Paso and find a children's hospital somewhere else. This was very stressful, both emotionally and financially for the families.

One of my colleagues from medical school and my first residency was married to a gal from El Paso, and she brought him back to El Paso. He became the first board-certified, fellowship-trained Pediatric Intensivist in El Paso. He came here in 2005-6, but the hospital didn't open until 2012. I had come back to El Paso in 2010, to work at an adult hospital where I could take care of children until the children's hospital was finished. At that point, there were only three of us who were board-certified Pediatric Intensivists in El Paso.

Lisette: How many pediatricians are at the hospital now?

Angie: I'm not sure of the number exactly, but the hospital has grown tremendously. We now have departments for endocrinology, pulmonology, cardiology, radiology, anesthesiology, oncology—the hospital has grown exponentially.

Lisette: Are you on the board of directors?

Angie: Oh no, I do not want to be part of the politics! (laughs)

Lisette: What does it mean to have that kind of hospital this close to the Mexican border? Are there immigrants who need help that might be afraid to seek care because of the fear of deportation?

Angie: The immigrants I see are very, very ill, but they get treated just like anyone else. They come from Mexico, Guatemala, and other Latin American countries, but even before our current problems with immigration, the kids who were hospitalized in Juarez would be driven by ambulance to the border, they'd get dropped off there, and then their parents would call 911. We are required by law to take them to the hospital, and since the hospital is a non-profit, it is designed to treat the whole community. These parents would risk their children's lives to get them to us, so the kids arrive extremely ill, and a lot of times we don't know what's been done to them in Mexico. They often did not get the right treatment and they are very sick—these are very complex situations.

Lisette: That is very complex! In those cases, how does that diagnostic process work, when these kids arrive without a background history?

Angie: It starts in the ER, and then several doctors have to make the diagnosis. We recently had an 18-year-old come in who had been diagnosed with leukemia. He had been wandering in the desert for two weeks traversing it, and he was so sick when he got to us, he was barely alive. He had no medical history that we knew of, and he had wandered into a smaller hospital outside of El Paso, and then they sent him to us. He was very, very ill, and he went straight into the operating room where they found he had leukemia. He was so lucky he didn't die enroute—he had been drinking water out of animal troughs to stay alive, he was so dehydrated and malnourished.

Barrett: But you saved him Angie, you did that, you saved a human life. You save lives every day.

Angie: Well, he almost didn't make it, but we found that he had relatives in New York, and that's where we sent him after he was stabilized.

Lisette: And all these immigrant kids who were separated from their parents at the border—is the hospital involved in treating any of them?

Angie: We take care of anyone who needs our help, that's part of our mission. Many of my colleagues volunteer to go see those kids at the border. They go see them in the shelters, and if they need to be admitted, there is a children's ward for them here. The ones I see in the ICU are already very, very sick.

Lisette: So the El Paso Children's Hospital is a non-profit, right? How does one actually start a non-profit hospital in the first place?

Angie: Well, there were some local pediatricians who were very active, and when they went to Austin, they managed to get the bill up for a vote. The city had to vote to approve the hospital, and it was a 120 million dollar endowment. The question was, do you want it or not? It was really a grassroots effort, and fortunately the people voted for it, because as a non-profit hospital, it serves the entire community.

Now, a lot of people were opposed to it too. They thought it would be overrun by illegal aliens, and the old hospital network didn't want to change things around, so there was actually a lot of marketing against it. But it really elevated the standards of pediatric care in West Texas, and the children's hospital is now so big that they recruit pediatric specialists from around the country. You know, a non-profit children's hospital does not make a lot of money, but you have to have children's hospitals like you need roads, like you need schools. You need healthy children to have a healthy community, and that creates jobs, so it's really about taking care of your people.

Lisette: So, you were one of the first three Pediatric Intensivists in El Paso. The city must have been excited to have you back after all those years away. Were you excited to come home?

Angie: Well, the hospital had already recruited me, and I knew I didn't want to work in an adult hospital anymore, so I was kept informed about the hospital bill's passage. And then when the construction began, that's when I moved back to El Paso. I had been gone exactly 20 years, plus or minus a month. It was both heartbreaking and transformative to leave Florida, but my life now is totally unrecognizable from before. At the time, I was going through a divorce, I was waiting for the hospital bill to pass, then the recruitment started, and then the building of the hospital began. So a lot of things had to fall into place—but it all worked out perfectly.

Barrett: How strange it is that there is such opposition to public health in our country, because we all know that a nation is only healthy as the individuals in that nation. I understand that your hospital operates as a non-profit, but after decades of experience as a doctor, what do you think is the best way to take care of people's health? Should we have some kind of social medicine, like Canada, Europe, and all the other developed nations? They seem to be doing much better than the US in terms of keeping their people healthy.

Angie: I think that most doctors fundamentally believe that all people should have access to health care. We just haven't figured out the best way to fund it, or the best way to approach it. It's an incredibly big issue, and I just don't know the answer, but we all generally believe that if you are sick, you should have access to health care. It's like shelter, food, healthcare, education, and safety—these are human rights. Every pediatrician I know feels the same way.

Lisette: The next generation of children is literally in your hands Angie!

Angie: Well, pediatricians are not the highest paid doctors, so we don't do it to become wealthy or famous. We look at a child and we say, yes, I want to take care of you! That's why we do it.

Lisette: Angie, your story is really quite incredible, and the common denominator we found with all of the women we interviewed for this book, is that each of them became who they are because of the struggles they faced as young women. They rose to overcome it, and they developed greatness in the process. Your story—it really sounds like a calling. How would you summarize the things that inspire you to do this work? What are your greatest joys in it?

Angie: A lot of my inspiration comes from my spiritual life with God. I cannot do this work without deep prayer for guidance, and for wisdom. I pray for my team, for myself, but I mostly pray that God protects the children from our own deficiencies. And I pray for the families, I really pray for their protection, because it's not about me. I go to work for the children with the common goal that they get better, so that they can go home. I pray for the complete recovery of the child and the family—I go big! The hospital is like a church for me, I am in constant prayer, and I pray that I have the courage to do what I need to do to make them better. I pray that I can do what the child needs, and if I can't, I pray that God will send the right doctor.

Lisette: There is a certain snag in that old system, which can make women feel like we are not capable or adept in our work. But then there is a moment when you realize that you are, indeed, totally capable. Did you have such a moment?

Angie: I don't know how to explain it, because it's tricky when it comes to medicine. There are some days when I know I did some good, I did something difficult, I led my team, and they felt proud, secure, and uplifted. I cannot allow my personal fears to spill over on to my team, and I have no choice but to be confident. My team might be ten nurses, a respiratory therapist, a physical therapist, a nutritionist, medical students, young doctors in training, and of course the families. You have to show them that you are actively looking for, and doing what is best for the child.

You know, I recently met a colleague who had just started working as a liaison between our hospitals, and it turned out that he was the same oncologist who treated me as a kid! And we were sitting there, and he hasn't seen me since I was about 14, and he said, "It's been about 30 years since I've seen you—how's your mom?" Consider that for a moment: here I am, 20 years after leaving El Paso, sitting across from my pediatric oncologist—not as his patient, but as his colleague.

That's when I knew, I was in the right place.

PODEROSAS

Carolyn Hartness

Eastern Band Cherokee & FASD Advocate

"When you were born, you cried and the world rejoiced. Live your life so that when you die, the world cries and you rejoice."

–*Cherokee Proverb*

Lisette: Carolyn Hartness was Barrett's first Indigenous spiritual teacher, and she's very special to both of us because she is also the one who married us. Barrett can you please introduce this incredibly powerful and generous woman? Tell us what you learned from her wisdom, and a little about the ceremony you are going to do with her.

Barrett: I first met Carolyn Hartness in 1995, when we attended a talk given by a visiting Maori *Tohunga* in Seattle. The Maori are the Indigenous Polynesian people of New Zealand who colonized the South Pacific, and their Tohungas are a kind of shaman or spiritual leader, the equivalent being something like a Native American medicine person. The Maori Tohungas carry a deep and ancient wisdom from countless generations of ancestors, and they are renowned for their powerful memories, which is what this particualr talk was about.

The teachings of Indigenous people can often be similar, or at least parallel to other teachings, and this is because of their unique understanding of the Earth and her ancient, natural energies. Indigenous people have always had a deep respect for their environments, the plants and animals that live in those ecosystems, and of course their own cultures, which have been around for tens of thousands of years. Hence, many Native American people from the Pacific Northwest were at this particular talk, and I had some New Zealand friends with me as well.

My New Zealand friends were musicians and writers, so when the Tohunga's talk concluded, they stepped up to speak with their Maori countryman, and I stood up to meet the people sitting in our row. To my right was a beautiful, Cherokee woman, about 20 years older than me, and striking in her appearance. She smiled at me, and I extended my hand to introduce myself. It was Carolyn Hartness, and thus began my decades-long friendship with this amazing teacher, who also became my first Indigenous mentor.

During the 1990s and still to this day, Carolyn is considered to be a global expert on Fetal Alcohol Spectrum Disorder (FASD), which is a condition that plagues many Indigenous mothers and their children. Indeed, FASD can affect mothers from any race when alcohol is consumed during pregnancy—the syndrome has no racial boundaries.

In tandem with her professional work with FASD, Carolyn is also a respected elder who leads various groups in the Northwest Native American community. During my time learning from her, I was able to participate in several traditional ceremonies, many of which we practiced at her beautiful home in the forest of the Kitsap Peninsula in Washington State, near the aptly titled village of Indianola. Most of the ceremonies we practiced were from the Lakota people, who were some of Carolyn's teachers as well. This is because of a conscious decision made by many Lakota elders a few generations back, to spread their wisdom teachings to any Native and non-Native peoples who wanted to learn their ways. That decision was based on prophecies experienced by their medicine people, who saw that the world was going to change dramatically, so it was important to share these wisdom teachings with the greater world.

It was a wise decision, because the Lakota now have many allies with both Indigenous and non-Indigenous people around the world, and this is evidenced in the support the Lakota received when they fought against oil developers at the Dakota Access Pipeline, and other places where Indigenous sovereignty has been threatened by corporate greed. Carolyn herself was mentored by one of the Lakota's most famous medicine men, the great Wallace Black Elk, and as a result of that wisdom generosity, Carolyn and her Lakota friends were willing to pass on some of that wisdom to me.

I've participated in the *Inipi* sweat lodge ceremony countless times, as well as the pipe ceremony, and even the great Sundance ceremony, where I refined my training on how to build and maintain the Sacred Fire. This became my most focused practice, because within fire-building are some of the most profound spiritual teachings I have ever experienced in my life, all of which I follow to this day.

Much of what I learned from Carolyn and other Native elders seemed intuitive to my own spiritual awareness, because my family had Cherokee ancestors and Native American spiritual practices were always close to my heart. The ceremonies are very grounded, yet they are also extremely beautiful to participate in. These were my first spiritual initiations, because there is nothing as powerful as building a fire, sweating it out in a sweatlodge to cleanse the heart and mind, drumming and singing, and of course, all the humor and laughter that Indigenous people are famous for.

In these ceremonies, I felt as if I could feel the spirit of the great Lakota warrior, Crazy Horse, and it was Carolyn who showed me that spirit. So for this conversation, we decided to split it into two parts, interspersed between an Inipi ceremony where I would build a Sacred Fire, and over a long dinner in Carolyn's beautiful home.

It is early November as we leave Seattle for Carolyn's home, and the morning is foggy and cool. I am looking forward to building the fire, but in order to do it correctly, I have to concentrate and remember each of the different steps in their proper sequence, the prayers that go with each part, and all of the details that make the difference between something being average, and something being truly powerful and transformative. Only the latter matters in this life.

I try to remember the prayers: South is the direction of the Child, its color is white, and all life emanates from this place. West is the direction of the Thunder Beings, its color is black, and from this place come the rains that cleanse us. North is the direction of the Wind, its color is red, and from this place come the storms, which both challenge and purify us. East is the direction of the Sun, its color is yellow, and from this place come the spirits, and all the wisdom they have to teach us....

Lisette: We arrive at Carolyn's house at almost exactly 6 am, the appointed time for Barrett to start building the fire before sunrise. Carolyn is in her kitchen with a couple other Native people who have come for the sweat lodge, arriving the night before. We say friendly hellos, refill our coffee, and Barrett loads the fire-building tools into Carolyn's truck—a couple of pitchforks, a double-headed axe, a rake, a bucket and ladle, and three large water containers. He also grabs newspaper and a red Bic lighter—the *Sacred Bic*, as they fondly refer to it, even though this is probably the 100th Bic lighter they've used over the years. It's cold outside, but it is totally clear, and a cobalt blue sky is emerging on the horizon.

We drive up the narrow road that connects Carolyn's house to her forested land a little higher up on the hillside where she, and a City of Seattle firefighter named Ben Dennis, have built a beautiful, cedar sweat lodge. It's a gorgeous place, thick with large maples, pine, hemlock, Douglas fir, and many thin alders, which elbow their way through the larger trees. We carry the tools down the narrow footpath to the lodge site and lean them against a large woodpile.

Barrett begins raking the area where he will build the fire. There are some pieces of charcoal left over from a previous ceremony a few months earlier, but because of the extremely dry summer, no fires have been built until now. Carolyn reminds him to save the largest pieces of charcoal and set them off to the side. "Those are the Elders, and they'll go back into the fire after we build the new one."

He rakes the fire pit smooth, slow and deliberately because, as Carolyn advises, "Slowly is holy", which I think is probably true for almost everything in life. There is no need to rush or do things carelessly, because when we do, we go off balance and make mistakes, sometimes hurting ourselves or others in the process. This is especially true when dealing with axes, pitchforks, and large fires. More importantly, slowing down the mind creates the space for spiritual awareness to emerge.

Carolyn tells Barrett to put aside 28 stones for the fire, and these are large, round basalt rocks, which are in the center of the lodge, left there after a previous lodge several months earlier. He pulls them out carefully, kneeling low as he extracts them, placing them in four neat rows of seven, one row of stones for each round of the lodge....

Carolyn, you're renowned for your work with Indigenous people throughout the United States, Canada, and even Australia and New Zealand. You told us earlier that the reintroduction of Indigenous ceremonies, especially for the children who suffer from FASD, has really helped them heal by reconnecting with their cultural identity. I've also heard you say that it is the *intention* in a ceremony that brings the real power to it, which makes all the difference for the participants. Can you explain how that intenitonal power actually works, and how it heals us?

Carolyn: Of course, so let's start with fire-building as an example. Barrett has created the sacred space for the fire, so let's have him pour some cornmeal on the ground, and we'll make an offering to the spirit of the fire. In doing so, we create reverence for the ceremony and the spirits that will protect us, and we place our intention on making it a powerful, healing ceremony for everyone involved. That's the intention creating the potential for healing, right at the beginning of the ceremony.

Lisette: Barrett makes the cornmeal design on the flattened earth, and then he lays out the first pieces of firewood to build the foundation of the fire, laying the wood end-to-end, pointing north/south, and then another row pointing east/west. This honors the four cardinal directions.

Now it's time to place the first five stones, one for each of the four directions, and one for the central axis that connects Earth and Sky. He then offers tobacco and more prayers to the four directions and the central axis, and then he starts stacking on the remaining 23 stones. It takes a fair bit of time to balance them correctly, as these are large, heavy stones. The fire structure is completed by laying the rest of the wood around the stones in a pyramid-like shape, after which he builds the four gates, where the spirits of the four directions will enter into the fire.

At this point, we have a large structure that is about 5 feet high and wide, and all the sacred elements have been added: cornmeal, wood, stone, tobacco, and most importantly, the prayers. The morning sky is clean and clear, and the sun is about to rise. The last element that needs to be added is the fire itself, which he lights in the East Gate. It is from the East, where the spirits of many different traditions like to enter.

We hear the whistle call of a bald eagle, a very good omen, and everyone pauses for a few seconds to listen. Did you hear that?

Carolyn: Yep, they usually show up right about now.

Lisette: Carolyn, why is the fire such an important part of Native American ceremonies, and what is its elemental power?

Carolyn: Well, fire is a living thing, and it reflects back on the spirit of the person building it, as well as the people doing the ceremony. The fire is the engine of it all, so you really have to have strong intention, remember the prayers, and most importantly what your reason is for doing the ceremony in the first place. Now you are seeing this in action—you focus your mind on the intention, you allow the healing energy to enter, and now we are going to have a very good sweat lodge.

Lisette: It ends up being a very large, very hot fire, and the narrow path around the center is barely wide enough for a person's body. You can singe yourself if you are not careful, if you are not mindful, and it reaches out and singes Barrett a few times.

Carolyn: That's the fire trying to connect with you, it just wants to thank you and touch you.

Lisette: It's now a roaring blaze, and we can see through the burning pyre that the 28 stones are glowing red with their internal fire-wisdom, as more wood is added on to keep the blaze going.

More people are starting to arrive for the sweat, most of whom Barrett has known for many years, from the countless ceremonies they have done in Carolyn's forest. All of them are very good, powerful beings, most of them four-year Sundancers with scars on their chests and arms from breaking from the Tree Of Life. These are tough people, and they are also deeply spiritual and wise.

They comment, "Great fire!," and we feel the heat from the embers as we intuit that it's going to be a very hot, powerful, and transformative sweat. It's now about 11 am, and the fire has been burning for almost four hours—the stones are ready, and there's a deep, grounded feeling amongst the attendees as they prepare to go into the lodge.

Barrett's last task is to pull sprigs off a cedar bough, which he burns in a coffee can using embers from the fire. It's a form of smudge, the smoke purifies the attendees as they arrive at the entrance of the lodge.

The smell of the smoke instantly takes me back to Buddhist ceremonies I had done years earlier, it's a universal smell, and I immediately feel cleansed as the smoke passes over and through my body. Carolyn calls to the group, "OK, let's go in," and so it begins.

After the lodge concludes a few hours later, we return to Carolyn's house to have a communal dinner of wild salmon, fresh salad and vegetables, and of course the pie and coffee that Barrett always brings. Later that evening, after the house has cleared out, we ask Carolyn the questions that most define her remarkable life.

Carolyn, thank you for all that you have done, and everything you have taught us. I first met you when you agreed to marry Barrett and I, and we couldn't be happier to be back here in your home, as you continue the teachings. Can we start by talking about your childhood, and how you began to understand and develop your identity as a mixed-blood Cherokee woman?

Carolyn: Well, my dad was Eastern Band Cherokee from North Carolina, but my mother was born here, and my grandmother was from Norway, so she only spoke Norwegian at home. My father treated me like a little boy, which was fine actually, I didn't mind it at all, and this made me very independent from an early age. I started working by about the time I was 12-years-old, doing all kinds of manual labor, from spring-cleaning people's houses, to mowing lawns and weeding gardens. That gave me the ability to leave home and live independently by the time I was about 17.

But my guidance counselor in high school told me not to aim too high, and she focused on the fact that my aptitude test in mechanics was the highest in the school, which was the result of all the hours I spent handling my father's tools. She didn't think I could use my mind academically, but fortunately my dad wanted me to go to college and not a trade school. So I applied to some universities, got accepted, and I became the first person in my family to receive a college education.

Lisette: That's exactly what my high school counselor said to me! "Don't aim too high, just look for a job as a secretary," she said. But unlike your father, my family agreed with my counselor, because in their minds, the goal was to have just enough skill to get by until I got married and had kids. It's a Mexican cultural thing.

Carolyn: Exactly! But you know, because I was raised to be independent, I learned pretty quickly that if you don't have your eyes open and ready to see an opportunity, you'll miss some of the big omens and big blessings that come your way—you'll miss the signs from the spirits! Sometimes you just know something at a very deep, intuitive level, and it can't be explained away with the intellect or the rational mind. That's the world of spirit moving in and around us, speaking to us, and that's why I wasn't afraid to leave home and start my own life at just 17.

Lisette: You have said that you were much more influenced by the Cherokee side of your family, which was your dad's side, but that you also loved the Norwegian influence, which came from your mother's side. How did those two cultural influences guide you into into a health and science field like Fetal Alcohol Spectrum Disorder? Were you working with Indigenous families at that point?

Carolyn: Well, I got into the University of Washington first, which was kind of rare for any Native woman back then, and I graduated with a Bachelor of Arts degree. Then I worked as the Director of Student Services for the College of Ocean and Fishery Sciences, which was a really fascinating job. I did that for many years, and then in the early 1990's, I started working for a Native American street youth program, where I learned about Fetal Alcohol Spectrum Disorder. After that, I began to work more independently with the local Indigenous tribes, and I started my FASD counseling business, something that was also not common for a Native woman back then.

But you know, I kind of learned early on that women are naturally better with business and money stuff, because we have been running households and managing our family affairs for thousands of years, all the way back to the earliest times. We ran the markets, the businesses, and we kept the communities together.

Lisette: That's right, women have been keeping families and communities together since the beginning of time. How did you find that power within yourself? You talked about how your father raised you as if you were a boy, and my father did the same with me, but you were also doing this ground-breaking healing work. When did that powerful self-image awaken?

Carolyn: When I was still pretty young, I began to realize that I had real power within me, but I was reluctant to be a leader, and I lacked a certain kind of self-confidence. Like my father, I wasn't taught our traditional Cherokee ways, so I kept looking for a teacher in the outside world who could do that. Much later in life, I met the Lakota medicine man, Wallace Black Elk, who I studied with for many years. I also worked with other spiritual teachers, including a man from Africa named, Dr. Bunseki Fu-Kiau. He came from the Congo in Central Africa and he taught a lot of people over here in the US. And you know, his teachings and Wallace's teaching were very similar, because they were both coming from a place of Indigenous wisdom. Wisdom is wisdom, so when they met in person, they were certain that their ancestors had been connected when the continents were closer together.

Barrett: I wish I could have met Wallace Black Elk, but I did meet Dr. Fu-Kiau a couple of times, once at your house, and once in New Mexico where he was giving a teaching. He was a very wise and spiritual man, and he exuded a deep calm that I distinctly remember. What was it like studying with Wallace Black Elk? I mean, his legacy is massive and is felt all over the world now.

Carolyn: I'll tell you a story about a sweat lodge ceremony that Wallace led, where a really remarkable thing happened. This will explain everything about his power.

Inside the lodge there were these fire spirits dancing on the inside of the roof, and it looked just as real as actual fire—but it wasn't. The next day I talked with one of Wallace's helpers about it, but he was just totally disinterested in what I was saying. I said, "Listen, you don't understand, the lodge was on fire!" He just said, "No, you don't understand— those are Wallace's fire spirits!" And that's when I realized that I didn't really know anything, and it was time for me to just be quiet and learn from these old, wise people and of course, the spirits.

I had to step back from my intellect, because I was trying to understand this spiritual power through my intellect, when in fact, it was all about the spirits working through the medicine people. Also because when the fire spirits first appeared inside that sweat lodge, Wallace shouted, "The eagle nation is speaking to this little girl!"—and he meant me.

Barrett: I've had experiences similar to that in sweat lodges, where the stones actually sang in polyphonic voices. That Indigenous power is very real, but it's not the way we've been taught, because it's so old and so ancient. In school, we're only taught about the most recent 500 years of colonial history, most of which is biased and incorrect. But the Indigenous cultures go back 20,000 years or more, yet we are taught very little about them. Our education system is so totally backwards, and we don't teach the real wisdom that we should be passing on to the next generations.

Carolyn: The world of spirit is very real, and it's huge. My biggest epiphany came when I realized that I could assist people with their healing. This happened when I was doing a sweat lodge for a young woman who had a rare, terminal form of cancer with no known cure. After the ceremony, this woman had her regular doctor appointment, during which she discovered her tumor had disappeared completely. Her doctors were in total disbelief, as there was no explanation for it. The woman disappeared for about a week, and we didn't hear from her the entire time. I thought she might still be sick, but then she finally called me on the phone and said, "Why do I get to live?" To which I replied, "That is your question to answer. It's a question each of us must answer. Why do we get to live, and what do we do with this life?"

Lisette: That's the big question right there—what do we do with the life we have been given?

Carolyn: Wallace said it best when he said, "The longest journey is from the head to the heart." And when you can do that, you'll know how to live your life.

Lisette: That is a beautiful and very wise statement, thank you for sharing it. The Tibetan Buddhists always point to their heart when they say, "Let me think about it," and I think it harkens to the process of moving aside, so that a deeper wisdom can emerge. How did you go from studying with Wallace Black Elk and Dr. Fu-Kiau, to your work with kids who suffer from FASD?

Carolyn: Well, FASD is one of the greatest problems affecting Indigenous people around the world, and really, it can affect anyone whose mother drinks alcohol during her pregnancy, regardless of their race. There is also research that suggests that a father's drinking can also create problems with the fetus. This includes drug use as well, and the result is that their children can be born with learning disabilities and sometimes facial malformations, such as the eyes being very widely set apart.

It really is the biggest plague on Indigenous people—the introduction of alcohol and drugs, which are chemical weapons that emerged in the wake of European and American colonial-capitalism. They stole Native lands from the people, and then supplanted their spiritual beliefs and ceremonies with alcohol and Christian missionaries who didn't know anything about the people or the cultures they were destroying.

Lisette: Yep, that is the real history that needs to be taught in schools and not hidden away from people. How did your Indigenous background shape your understanding of the dynamics between women and men?

Carolyn: Well, the Cherokee influence came from my father's side, but his mother didn't want to teach us anything, so the vast majority of my training came from working with Lakota people, as well as numerous other Native peoples around the Pacific Northwest and Canada. And in many of those cultures, the women have an equal or even greater say in things, because they came from matriarchal cultures. I just sat and listened to what they had to say to me.

You know, men have this age-old belief that the early hunter-gatherers were responsible for feeding the tribal unit, but this is a completely and totally false myth. Yes, men found meat through hunting and fishing, but in fact, this was a relatively small amount of the caloric intake for the tribe. Meat was really more of a luxury and not the main form of subsistence. The overwhelming amount of calories consumed by the tribe was gathered and grown by the women—the grandmothers, mothers, and daughters, who gathered wild vegetables, fruits, nuts, and eventually learned to bake breads. Meat was enjoyed when it was available, but as far as feeding the family unit, it was the women who shouldered that burden, as in, like, they literally carried the food on their shoulders!

Lisette: Right! And I would argue that this belief is not only held by men, but also by women to a certain extent, because women are only deemed successful if they can think and act like men. The metric is completely askew, but our strength is something much different, no?

Carolyn: Women just think differently than men do, and this is a fact, so men shouldn't try to think like women either. In the not so distant past, men had the job of hunting and bringing back the meat, and also protecting the people. The women's job was to hold the tribe together, feed the families, and keep the peace between the other tribes.

With colonization and the creation of these so-called jobs for wages, the traditional men lost their role as hunter-protector, and that's when violence began to emerge in the tribes. This includes the horizontal violence against their wives, their children, other family members, and with other men in their tribe.

And then with the introduction of alcohol, drugs, and low quality foods and sugar products, we saw the emergence of alcoholism, addiction, diabetes, and other Western diseases. Native people stopped eating their traditional foods and they started eating these refined, junk foods. In fact, those foods are not very good for anyone to eat, Indigenous or otherwise.

Lisette: Where then, do you think the image of feminine impotency began, this belief that only the men knew how to do things and the women were helpless?

Carolyn: Women started to be raised to think they were not competent anymore, which is a projection of that male insecurity. It is the fear of not being able to hunt, of not feeling needed, of not being allowed to do their traditional ceremonies, which many of the colonists and missionaries outlawed. Many Native ceremonies were only recently allowed to happen again, like the Sundance ceremony, which federal law prohibited until the late 1970s.

But remember, Indigenous cultures around the world are largely matriarchal, so the women are the original land holders and name owners. The introduction of Western drugs and alcohol created domestic violence, especially when the men lost their jobs and could not, or forgot, how to hunt and protect their families. The women, however, were still the same, they were still wives, mothers, and they didn't lose their cultural position. But the men did, and that was devastating for them, and the greater culture.

Barrett: I have seen so much alcholism and addiction, in my friends and band members who died from overdoses. It felt like a curse for a time, but then I saw that it was a cultural phenomena in America. We are such an addictive society, whether it's alcohol, drugs, food, sex, social media—basically anything we can do to excess, we will do it to excess. You don't have to be a rock star to be an addict—addiction is now across every age and demographic in this country.

Carolyn: The 2013 National Survey on Drug Use and Health (NSDUH) showed that 12.3% of American Indians were current users of illicit drugs, compared with 9.5% of Whites, 8.8% of Hispanics, and 10.5% of African Americans. The rate of binge drinking among American Indians was 23.5% and the rate of tobacco use was 40.1%. When your culture and your livelihood is taken away, the people become lost and they turn to escape through drugs and alcohol, and that just creates more violence and more fracturing. This is true with all Indigenous cultures, and it's certainly true with so-called American culture, which has devolved into a culture of consumption.

Lisette: The Indigenous perspective really explains the problems between men and women today, and particularly the way in which corporate America separates and divides the essential powers of men and women. It started with the colonists and missionaries, but now it's in the corporations—it brings out the worst in people's character. It's not how we were meant to live as spiritual-biological creatures.

Barrett: Totally, and let's not forget that the early colonial trading company is essentially what a modern-day corporation is modeled after. Corporate America has always been focused on profit at the expense of the environment, human rights, and even human life. As a result, they have developed a very myopic, self-rationalizing belief system that supports this exploitive worldview.

Carolyn: Man has essentially, for the last 2,000 years, had this sense of entitlement that they created the world as it is. Which, if you want to count the destruction of the environment, polluting the air, the land, the water, creating endless wars, then yes, the men made all of those things too. Fossil fuels, machine guns, atomic bombs, addictive drugs—they figured out how to make all of that destruction for profit. That is the modern, Western worldview, in a nutshell. The Indigenous worldview, by contrast, is more about preserving the collective, rather than rewarding the individual. It seeks holism rather than divisiveness.

Lisette: What is the correction then, what can we do to bring things back into balance?

Carolyn: I believe that there is a universal voice that speaks the same spiritual truths through many different messengers, throughout all of the world's cultures. It manifests in the different religions and spiritual practices, and these universal truths are generally the same: be good to one another, take care of the Earth, and live a simple life with a strong spiritual practice.

We have examples of this in our male leaders too, it's just not recognized as quickly. For example, we say that the best leaders lead from behind—that's what Sitting Bull and Crazy Horse did, and they are considered to be the greatest warriors and holy men in Lakota history. Sitting Bull was famous for literally riding at the back of his tribe's column, making sure the elderly people were keeping up, and that the children didn't wander off and get lost. He led and protected his people by example, leading them from a place of humility and grace.

Lisette: It's so true—the best American leaders were like those Native American chiefs or the leaders of the Civil Rights Movement. They were true American warriors, and they always led by example, far more than any current politician, that's for sure.

Carolyn: You know, real healing starts with the children, and I feel like the next generation that is growing up is pretty awake. They are very aware that everything is wrong in the world, and how dysfunctional we have become as a society. Our society is not running on love, it is running on fear—and fear breeds hate.

Lisette: On our most recent trip to Alaska, we had the honor of attending Quyana Nights, which is a huge music and dance performance, which features dozens of Alaskan Native groups. We interviewed an Indigenous Tlingit women who is a professor at the University of Alaska, and we were so impressed by the Native youth. They are actively learning their original languages, and the various songs and dances that go with their ceremonies—ceremonies that their parents were not allowed to practice in the mandatory boarding schools they had been forced to attend.

Barrett: Exactly, it was is as if the elders had held on just long enough for that next generation to catch up and make the hand off— it was magical to witness that process in real time. Indigenous people have this deep, ancient understanding of nature in a way that Western society generally lacks, because we've been overtaken by consumption. But consumption is not a culture, addiction is not a culture, and people are starting to realize that capitalism is a financial trap. These kids don't want to be trapped anymore, they want their cultures back.

Lisette: That's right, because we both taught young people from the Millennial Generation when we were professors, and we discovered that they intuitively knew that it was not acceptable to be a racist, or a bigot, or a homophobe—it just wasn't acceptable to be like that, in any way. I went away from my teaching experience feeling pretty good about the world's future, because I feel like these next couple of generations will be the ones who save our world from the old, racist, tyrants we are currently dealing with. I really believe they can do it—I mean, they sort of have to.

Carolyn: I think they will too, and the movement we see happening today is about women taking back their power. Men have been in power for far too long and it's just not working for anyone, except the super-rich who already benefitted from this patriarchy. We've lost our balance, and reclaiming our power is a process, but it's not an easy one. However ceremony and the world of spirit are here, waiting for us to ask them for help—and they show up when you ask them!

You know, I was once asked to do a particular kind of Lakota healing ceremony, but I didn't know exactly how to do it. I had just never been taught how to do it before, so I called Wallace Black Elk for help and he said, "Oh, you just weren't taught the specifics. Go grab a pen and paper and follow these instructions—I'm sure you can do it!"

That's all it is. We just need to help each other, feed each other, and teach each other. They always tried to defeat us by dividing us, but they could never do it, because the real power is in the community, and in the children.

And it's the children who are going to save us.

Magdalena & Edith Agustin

Shipibo Shamans & Traditional Healers In The Peruvian Amazon

"The Shipibo Shamans see it as our personal responsibility to heal anyone who comes to us for help. No matter who they are, from any part of the world, we will help them."

–Herlinda Agustin

Lisette: The first trip that Barrett and I made in our quest to interview powerful women, came when we visited the singing Shipibo Shamans of the Peruvian Amazon Rainforest. It was partly because we both love Peru for its unique place at the center of the old Inca Empire, but also because Barrett had previously done fieldwork with the Shipibo when he was in graduate school in the early 2000s. We were long overdue for a visit, thus, our first research trip for this book resulted in this story about one of the most magical cultures on Earth.

Peru is a nation imbued with deep wisdom, powerful medicine, and an ancient history, most of it carried by the Indigenous women from both the highland and lowland cultures. These societies are matriarchal, meaning they are guided by feminine wisdom, which is felt in the Quechua cultures of the Andes Mountains, just as it is with the Shipibo and other tribes throughout the Amazon Basin. Their wisdom teachings are some of the oldest in the world.

The Shipibo Shamans in particular, are globally renowned as masters of herbal and plant-based medicine, as well as for their exquisite singing, which includes sacred healing songs known as *Icaros*. The combination of these Icaros, in tandem with the medicines gathered and refined in the rainforest, is why people from all over the world seek the Shipibo for physical, emotional, and spiritual healing.

The Shipibo are also an extremely influential tribal group, and because of their unique location at the headwaters of the Amazon River, their animist philosophy extends well beyond their tribal area. Animism suggests that everything has a spirit, meaning that every human, animal, bird, plant, insect, and even the natural elements of earth, fire, water, thunder, lightning, and wind all have a spiritual essence to them. This is also what Buddhism, Taosim, and Zen essentially teach—that everything is equal in it's potential, despite being unique in its manifestation.

There are shamanic-animistic cultures all over the world, in fact, North and South America, Europe, Africa, Asia, and Australia all had Indigenous cultures with some form of animism in their origin. Many people relate to animism and the practice of shamanism for the same singular reason—it works, and when you experience it's power, there's no denying that these principles are real. What makes the Shipibo so powerful is that their shamans tend to be women, in a process by which the grandmothers pass on their wisdom to their daughters and granddaughters. There are male shamans too of course, but the majority of the power lies with the women throughout the Upper Amazon.

On our recent visit, Barrett found the Shipibo to be very much the same as he remembered them, but also different in other ways. They've become modernized with the advent of the Internet, email, and smartphones, to the degree that we are now connected on social media. Some of them were just children when Barrett first visited in 2004, but almost all of them now have children of their own.

We wanted to talk with the Shipibo about how globalization and the Internet is affecting their traditional way of life, and also how they are managing their cultural economy during the global climate crisis, the fires of which are literally threatening the very heart of the Amazon Rainforest. Fortunately, people from all over the world continue to visit the Shipibo, to be healed by them, to hear their beautiful singing, and to purchase one of the most unique forms of musical-spiritual expression ever created—the Shipibo song cloth. Our conversations with the Shipibo women span these subjects, as well as the protection of the Amazon Rainforest, and the ancient and magnificent Shipibo culture.

After three weeks living with our extended Shipibo family in 2018, including two years of regular communication via email and social media, I can personally call them family members. They are kind, joyous, pure, and spiritually-attuned people in a way that the world needs now more than ever. Barrett, will you please explain more about this, and your work with the Shipibo, as we set up the rest of this story?

Barrett: I did my graduate fieldwork in anthropology with the Shipibo Shamans starting in 2004, here in the main village of San Francisco de Yarina Cocha. My experience with the Shipibo was a singularly powerful experience in my life, one that dramatically changed the course of my work as a professional musician, and as an advocate for Indigenous cultures everywhere. You see, people from around the world seek out the Shipibo for their renowned healing abilities and their incredible singing, and this was the focus of my research.

During our time working together, which spanned between 2004-2006, I bonded closely with the extended Agustin family, and I recorded an album of their healing Icaros titled, "Woven Songs Of The Amazon: Healing Icaros Of The Shipibo Shamans." Lisette and I recorded another album of their Icaros on this 2018 trip titled, "Woven Songs Of The Amazon II: A Ceremony Of Healing With The Shipibo Shamans." Both of these albums are available worldwide as streaming and digital downloads, and 100% of the royalties go to these incredible healers.

This kind of musical-shamanism is an extremely powerful healing modality, and it can be understood through a three-tiered principle known as the *shamanic complex*, which can best be described like this:

1. The first principle, and the foundation of the complex, is based on the shaman's belief in their training, the effectiveness of their techniques, and their ability to heal others.

2. The second principle is the patient's belief in the shaman, the shaman's power, and the ability of the shaman to heal the patient.

3. The third principle is the faith and expectations of the larger community, which collectively believes in the shaman's power, and the shaman's ability to heal individuals withing the greater societal group.

All three of these principles work together to create a kind of gravitational field, within which the healing relationship between the shaman and patient is defined.

The Shipibo speak an Indigenous dialect known as Panoan, which is the main language group of the Upper Peruvian Amazon. However, they also speak Spanish and occasionally Portuguese, which is a result of the Peruvian governments' language programs, which are taught in regional schools throughout the Amazon, much like the one here in Yarina Cocha. Since Spanish is Lisette's first language, and I can understand it much better than I can speak it, we were able to converse with the Shipibo fluently and with ease, as our conversation will show.

Shipibo cosmology is largely centered around the belief that sacred singing can be used in tandem with natural medicines derived from the rainforest. The singing of the sacred Icaros, which the shamans hear from the spirits of the rainforest, is replicated in their mind through a process called *synesthesia*. This is how the shamans can *see* the patterns of the rainforest, which are represented by the *songlines* in the visual cortex of their minds.

The word Icaro itself seems to be a Castilianism derived from the Quechua verb *Ikaray*, which means, *to blow smoke in order to heal*. Like an incantation, the Icaro song patterns are deemed to be more powerful when they are woven into fabric, thus, the shamans weave and embroider these intricate songlines into their clothing, they paint them on their pottery and on the walls of their homes, and they sometimes paint them on their faces and bodies. In doing so, the Shipibo have created one of the most unique and compelling systems of healing in the world—a woven song healing tradition that goes back thousands of years.

This was what my research was centered around back in 2004-2006, but it barely scratched the surface of the incredible wisdom and powerful healing abilities of these shamans. That is why we are here, 14 years later, to have that conversation again, and to continue to learn.

The conversations for this story took place in the village of San Francisco de Yarina Cocha, or *serpent lagoon* as it is known locally. It is named as such because of the large anacondas that swim in these waters, which the Shipibo revere as their divine protector. We are about an hour up river from the frontier town of Pucallpa, on the banks of the wide and slow-moving Ucayali River, an upper tributary of the mighty Amazon.

The village has grown to almost 2,000 people (or shrunk, depending on who you ask) and this is the largest of the hundred or so Shipibo villages that are scattered throughout the Upper Peruvian Amazon. As we arrive, we walk along a modern, newly-built boardwalk of sorts, which takes us from the boat landing, up to the entrance of the village. The rest of the structures, however, seem very traditional: thatched-roof, open-air bungalows line the pink, dirt roads, their walls painted with the iconic Shipibo songlines. Children are playing in the earthen courtyards that demarcate the center of every compound, and the occasional car (which doubles as a taxi) are so rare and infrequent that the village is essentially silent. Aside from the occasional barking dog or laughing child, most of the sounds are coming from the cacophony of birds and insects that are constantly churning in the rainforest, and even that feels normal after a while, once the ear acclimates to it. In general, the whole village seems to be in a perpetual state of siesta.

Lisette: Our accommodations here are simple and spartan—we're staying in a single longhouse that adjoins another longhouse in an L-shape configuration, with a grass lawn in the middle. We are staying in the guesthouse, and we each have a hammock, which we cover with mosquito netting that we bought in Pucallpa. We've also brought two of our closest friends along with us: the artist and activist Erin Currier, who is interviewed at the end of this book, and Jeanine Debar, a dynamic, award-winning business woman from New York City.

The shamans and their extended families live in bungalows that lie along the periphery of the earthen street, but we all gather every morning and evening for food and coffee, which is cooked and brewed in the adjoining longhouse. This is where four generations of shamans, their children, their grandchildren, and even a few great-grandchildren all sit together, eat together, tell stories, and most importantly, sing and laugh. This is where most of our conversations take place.

When Barrett was here in 2004, the main matriarch of the village was the highly revered shaman, Herlinda Agustin, the wife of the equally revered shaman and *Ayahuascero*, Enrique Sinuiri. Unfortunately, Herlinda passed away in the interim years, and along with her went an incredible repertoire of healing Icaros. Her absence, both spiritually and physically, is represented poignantly in the painted portrait that hangs on the largest wall of the main longhouse.

Under Herlinda's watchful, painted eyes, her children and grandchildren eat, talk, play, and occasionally sell a woven song cloth to a passing tourist. It's a kind of pop-up shop that the Shipibo have created at the far end of the longhouse, so that when a tourist does happen to walk by, the shamans are ready to sell their beautiful weavings, ceramics, and jewelry, perhaps singing an Icaro or two to seal the deal. These sales, while financially small, make a huge difference in the day-to-day lives of these women, as they raise their children and hopefully send them to school.

We have been in the village for about a week now, the requisite amount of time needed to maintain a *dieta* to purify the body before doing the powerful *Ayahuasca* ceremony. We completed the dieta, but I had reserved the right not to do the ceremony—being from New York I had known of many people who had been deeply damaged by Ayahuasca brought to the city and administered by people who weren't real shamans. However, here in the Peruvian Amazon, the home of the Ayahuasca vine and leaf, I was willing to consider it.

On the day of the ceremony, we continue the dieta and spend the day with the Agustin family, walking in the forest and around their sacred *maloka*, a traditional round house used for ceremonies. We are taken to Herlinda's garden grave where the family claims to see and communicate with her still, and I believe them, because I feel her too—some part of me hears her voice piercing through the veil between the realms. The sounds of the birds and insects grows louder and louder as the sun begins to set, and we all begin to gather with our blankets in the maloka—it's an all night ceremony after all.

The rainforest at dusk is as loud as a sawmill full of insects, and there is one bug in particular that is much louder than all the rest. It makes us laugh with its comedic chirping, and I notice that the whole maloka is filled with the laughter of children, as the Agustin family members greet each other, and us, as they find their place on the huge wooden floor. They are such happy people, and their eyes shine with great joy as they dance, and play, and joke around with us. We are sitting in a large circle as we wait for the ceremony to begin.

Herlinda's widower, Enrique, is leading the ceremony tonight, and I don't doubt that he has conjured the spirit of his beloved wife and asked her to join us. Enrique has a profound presence about him, yet his kind smile puts us all at ease—tonight he sets aside his baseball cap and denim jeans in lieu of white robes, the regalia of a true Ayahuascero. I'm watching everyone, I see a baby crawling across the floor towards her mother, and I'm waiting for a formal beginning. Soon Enrique is standing before me and he offers me a cup. I ask him what it is, to which he replies, "This is the medicine of our land. I've made it very gentle for you because this is your first time, but I will give you more if you want it later." The laughter, the familial joy, and the kindness in his eyes was all I needed to know that I would be safe. "The rainforest will always be a part of you now," he says as I drink from the cup.

We each had very different experiences during the ceremony that night, and on the following nights. Mine were full of primordial awakenings, visions of the patterns that the shaman-weavers capture, and the songs that draw the spirit of the anaconda and the jaguar. Enrique was right, I did have the rainforest within me, and hereafter I always will. It's this connection to the Earth that the modern world has lost, but once we are reconnected, protecting it becomes obligatory. We sleep on the hard wooden floors, and like the vine medicine that we drank, we wind our way through the land in our sleep, Herlinda's voice bridging the divide....

The next day we begin our conversation for the book, and it has been left to Herlinda's daughter, Magdalena, and Magdalena's daughter, Edith, to carry on the family tradition of singing, weaving, healing, and teaching. It is around these two powerful women-shamans that our story is centered.

Magdalena, it is such an honor to finally meet you after hearing about you through Barrett, and listening to the recordings of your beauitful singing! Can you please tell us about the Shipibo tradition of singing the songs of the rainforest—the sacred Icaros? How was this tradition passed on to you?

Magdalena: Lisette, we are so happy to have you and Martin back here with us—14 years is much too long! First, let me tell you our creation story about the Great Anaconda, Ronin, as this explains much about our singing. It was she who created the Shipibo universe.

In this story, Ronin is in total darkness, and she is circling the Tree of Life, making a giant circle as wide as the universe. As she comes around to see her entire body, she sees the beautiful designs on her skin, and this makes her so happy that she begins to sing out all the patterns that she sees. Her singing created the sun, the moon, the stars, the Earth, and all of the creatures that live within these realms, and that is why everything has its own song. This is how the world was created, through singing, and when we listen carefully, we can hear the Icaros of the rainforest singing to us.

We have memorized many of these Icaros, and my mother and grandmother also taught them to me. When someone becomes sick, we can see that their personal song is all tangled up, like a string with many knots. We can actually see the songline in their body, and it glows with a white light, but when they are sick, the songline gets all tangled up. When we start singing the sacred Icaros, the knots start to untangle, and we can bring their body and spirit back into balance. Sometimes we also make *piri piri* (herb-based medicine) to help with the sickness, but it's mostly the singing that heals the soul. All sicknesses come from these imbalances in the body, and doctors know this too. We just heal people in the ancient way—with songs and plants from the rainforest.

Barrett: Magdalena, it's been 14 years since we've seen each other, but if you remember, I flew your mom and dad up to New Mexico in 2005 to teach at the University of New Mexico. I recorded more of their Icaros there, and I'll play those recordings for you later, but please tell us—what is going on in the village now that Herlinda has passed away? She was working with people from all over the world when I was here, teaching and healing them in the Shipibo way. Are you still working with people from other countries, and are they still coming here?

Magdalena: Yes they are still coming here, but it was terrible when my mother died. We feel her spirit around the village all the time, and she still comes to the ceremonies to be with her family. But I have my own maloka now, we named it the Maloka Puma Negra (Black Puma Healing Center), and it has a teaching center too. My oldest daughter, Katy, was only 14-years-old when you were last here, and she is now a college student in Lima. She is setting up a new website to let people know all the ways we can help them, how they can get here and find us, and all the various things we are teaching about Shipibo culture.

Lisette: Magdalena, can you tell us how you hear the Icaros in the rainforest, and how you weave them into a song cloth? Is there a special technique that you follow?

Magdalena: I first started learning the Icaros when I was about 8-years-old. I heard them from my grandmother, Manuela, who also taught me how to weave the traditional, woven patterns that represent the Icaros. Over time, I learned how to weave the more modern, complex designs, and we have a saying that the best weavers are also the best singers. My mother's weavings were really incredible—everyone wants her old weavings now because no one can duplicate them. That's why she was the best singer and the most powerful shaman in the entire district.

The Icaros can also come from walking in the rainforest and just listening to what the spirits want to teach you—but you have to listen! They can also come in dreams, and they always come during the Ayahuasca ceremonies. Sometimes, an old female ancestor comes to me in my dreams, and she teaches me new Icaros and she shows me new song patterns. I usually hear the song first, and then the pattern emerges in my mind. I hear them, then I see them—they just come to me.

Lisette: And Edith, how do you hear the songs, and how do you see the song patterns?

Edith: I'm learning a lot of Icaros from the older shamans, and I'm also learning how to weave them into song cloths. It's a long process! I first started hearing them from my grandparents, Herlinda and Enrique, and also from my mother, but I am now learning them on my own, listening to the rainforest, and also in my dreams.

Barrett: Edith, you were just a little girl when I was here before! You were telling me yesterday, when we were recording your Icaros that you are also doing more modern singing, where you sing Icaros with a DJ from Lima. How do you like mixing electronic music with the modern version of Icaros? And you're doing live shows too—what is it like to perform them for an audience?

Edith: It's really fun! I sing the Icaros and the DJ puts a beat and electronic sounds to them, and then we make them into new recordings. We've played some live shows together in Lima, and people really like the mixing of the old traditional singing with the modern electronic music. It's inspiring to see that people in the city really appreciate Shipibo music and culture—it makes me proud to be Shipibo!

Lisette: Edith, how do the song cloths actually heal people?

Edith: The song cloth represents the physical manifestation of the Icaro woven into a pattern, and it contains all of the healing power and medicinal properties of the plant or animal for which it is associated. The Icaro contains the name of the plant, animal, or spirit for which it gets its power, it tells us how that medicine will work on certain illnesses, and it tells us how it will heal the patient. When we honor the spirit for its curing and healing abilities, it *wants* to heal the person, it is compelled to heal them. After it has done its work, we thank the spirit generously so it will come back again.

The song cloths are the physical embodiment of the Icaros healing power, so we weave song cloths for all of them: the Anaconda, the Ayahuasca, the Hummingbird, the Puma, the Dolphin, the Rainforest, the Water—anything that is called upon to heal, we have an Icaro and a song cloth that works together to heal the person.

Lisette: Magdalena, you have three grown children now, and it seems like there are a lot of new babies and little ones running around the village. How do you prepare them for the Shipibo way of healing?

Magdalena: When a baby is in the womb, we sing a lot of Icaros to prepare it to be received into the world. For the first few months, the fetus is just doing what it needs to do, building it's body for the spirit to enter. At a certain point, sometime between the 6th and 8th month, the spirit of the child enters the fetus, and the mother can feel it. Sometimes the mother will go sit in front of an Ayahuascero to find out the health and gender of the baby, and the Ayahuascero can see the baby like a picture in their mind. During this whole period of time, we are singing Icaros to the baby, to welcome it, and to keep it protected in the womb until it is born.

You probably noticed that most of the women in the village are wearing a white skirt with colorful songlines on them? These are the patterns for the Wisdom Icaro and the Protection Icaro. We wear these skirts because, in our culture, the women carry the wisdom and the power to protect, and that is especially true when we are bringing a new child into the world.

Barrett: I remember when I was here in 2004, I bought a lot of those wisdom skirts for the women in my family. And during that time, there was a birth in a house just down the street from here. I was walking past the house, and there were about 20 people standing around, children peering through the windows, and the adults were looking very concerned. It was obvious from the sounds coming from within that a woman was in labor. One of the midwives asked me to take a message to Herlinda, that the mother was having a lot of difficulty with the birth. I walked back to Herlinda's house and gave her the message—she just went inside and shut the door. About 20 minutes later, she emerged to inform us that the birth had happened without any complications. Sure enough, we got news that the mother had a healthy baby, simultaneous to Herlinda's magic.

Lisette: I heard someone say that there a special song cloth that is made for the babies before they are born? Can you describe that?

Magdalena: Yes, exactly! My grandmother, my mother, and I all received Icaros from our children when they were still in the womb. Their songs would come to us in dreams, complete with their individual songlines, which we would weave into a song cloth and sing in anticipation of their birth. These pregnancy cloths are sometimes worn as skirts, or simply placed over the belly to protect the baby and ensure its health. Then we take that song cloth and use it as the actual birthing cloth, wrapping the baby in it immediately after it's born. The cloth imprints the Icaro on the baby, and protects it with its own songline.

Lisette: That is just incredible Magdalena, I've never heard a story as beautiful as that, for bringing new life into the world. Barrett and I were born in sterilized hospitals where we got slapped on the bottom, and nobody sang to us! (everyone laughs)

Barrett: I was born at 5 pm, at the start of Happy Hour, and my dad said they all left the hospital to go have cocktails! This explains everything.... (laughing continues)

Lisette: Can you tell us more about the use of the Icaro designs, especially when you paint them on your face and body?

Magdalena: Yes, when we want to put the power of the Icaro right into the body, we use a kind of ink called *Huito*. The Huito is made from boiling the seeds of a certain fruit from the rainforest, which produces a dark, blue-black ink. It has been used for many generations, and it serves several functions, including as a shampoo, which dyes our hair black, and it can also be used as a purgative to clean out intestinal problems. Mostly we use it to paint the Icaro patterns on the face and body, using a small stick like a paintbrush. It looks like a tattoo, but it washes off after a few days.

We often do this for healing rituals, like if someone has injured a part of their body, then we use the Huito to draw songlines on that part of the body. These patterns are very intricate, like the patterns on the song cloths, so it takes a long time to paint them.

Barrett: I remember watching Herlinda make Huito. She scraped the seeds out of a melon fruit, boiled it until it was black, and then she painted the designs on the back of a photographer who was with us—he had broken his spine in a car accident many years earlier, and he always suffered from back pain. He swore that after Herlinda worked on him, he was healed and didn't have any pain after that.

I also remember Herlinda showing us all the medicinal plants in her garden, and all the things she could heal with them. Can you talk about those plants?

Magdalena: We still use my mother's garden, and it has many plants and herbs that heal all sorts of things. Things like high blood pressure, diabetes, various heart problems, circulation problems, digestive problems, and even man and woman problems! (everyone laughs)

Lisette: What about the Ayahuasca ceremony, can you tell us more about that? Ayahuasca wasn't very well known in the outside world until farily recently, and this is the first time I have ever taken it, here with your family. Now everyone talks about Ayahuasca as the miracle cure for everything, and people are doing it in New York City, although I would never want to do it there. It seems like the Amazon Rainforest is the best place to do it, since it is grown here and made here—and only with a real Shipibo Shaman.

Magdalena: Of course, we do the Ayahuasca ceremony for people when they come here to be healed and to learn from us. But there are a lot of false shamans out there now, who claim to understand the power of the Ayahuasca, but they don't, and that's when it can be very dangerous. You should only do Ayahuasca with a trained Shipibo Shaman, or a true Ayahuascero. Otherwise, many things can go wrong.

The ceremony itself is an all-night ceremony that we use for receiving visions, and for the spiritual and physical healing of an individual, which are usually intertwined. My mother always said that the Shipibo saw it as their personal responsibility to heal anyone who comes to us, from anywhere in the world, and quite often, someone from a far-away country will show up at the river's edge asking for a local shaman, and they are never turned away. We see this as our sacred duty as Shipibo people, as Shipibo Shamans.

Lisette: Edith, your grandmother, Herlinda, said the Shipibo are here to heal people from all over the world—this is your sacred duty. And now you have the Maloka Puma Negra, where people can find your music, your weavings, and participate in ceremonies for the Shipibo way of healing. What else do you want the people who read this book to know about your work?

Edith: Well, first I want to say to Martin, when you make our next album, please don't make any CDs this time, OK? Nobody buys CDs anymore, especially out here in the rainforest! (everyone laughs) Just make it a digital album, and then everyone around the world can hear it. Also, please tell them to come here and learn from us directly—that is the best way to learn the Shipibo ways.

Magdalena: I still remember when my parents had vinyl LPs that we listened to a long time ago, and then we had some CDs, and now we are in a new kind of digital world. It's good though, more people can find us on the Internet, and we can teach them about the power of the rainforest. The rainforest is here to teach all of us, and that is why we must protect it.

But you know, the Peruvian government has called us "savages" in the news, in an attempt to make us sound primitive and incapable of managing our lands. The government just wants to redistrict our rainforest and sell it off to the highst bidder, like they are doing in Brazil, where they are burning the rainforest to the ground.

We have been in this rainforest for tens of thousands of years, we understand how it works better than any government official or scientist, and we are certainly not primitive. We understand the forest's ancient systems, and the spiritual way that it teaches us. That's why people come from all over the world to be healed by the Shipibo.

Lisette: Indeed, these parting words are truer now in 2020 than they were when we visited in 2018. As we wind down our last evening in the village, we all eat dinner together, and we listen to a local radio station that broadcasts continuous Icaros, the words of which are being written down by Magdalena's husband, Bernardo, who is also a shaman and school teacher at the local government school. He sits at the large dining table and transcribes the words coming through the tiny radio, and it's that same beautiful, acapella singing that the Shipibo Shamans have made famous in this part of the world.

The children gather around and listen too, and we are reminded that Indigenous wisdom is not so much about honoring an ancient system simply because it is old—it is more about honoring a system that has been proven to work, and is still very much alive.

It's also about the wisdom teachings of the elders, and the countless generations of people who have lived so closely to the Earth and the rainforest, that they have come to know her deepest secrets and hidden mysteries.

It's also about the next generation of Shipibo children, who carry the sacred Icaros in their hearts, learning how to sing them, weave them, and how to heal others with their songs and traditional medicine.

All of the Shipibo carry this kind of wisdom, with a deep knowledge and reverence for the Amazon Rainforest and all of the plants and animals that live within it. We just happen to be fortunate in that this particular family of Shipibo Shamans has the ability to sing that wisdom to the world.

They do it for all of us, whether we are aware of it, or not.

THE TEACHERS

Dr. Robin Root

Medical Anthropologist & Situational Feminist

"Never doubt that a small group of thoughtful, committed, citizens can change the world. Indeed, it is the only thing that ever has."
                                                                                    –Margaret Mead

Lisette: I moved to New York City in 2001 with my friend, Dr. Robin Root—we were a bit like Thelma and Louise, actually. If I had to describe her in one sentence, I would say that she was born for the *Great Fight,* and that she delights in it. We were working for the same organization, the Phelps Stokes Fund, and we were trying to find our own way in that big city. It was just after the September 11th attack, and our office, which was situated on the same block as the World Trade Center, was filled with ash and debris and wouldn't re-open until February of the following year.

I lived in a great railroad apartment on 52nd Street, and Robin lived on the Upper Westside. I often walked to her part of town, and we shared many great times together, many of them over meals.

In January of 2002, I had begun work as an adjunct professor at John Jay College of Criminal Justice, and up until the last days of March that year, Robin and I were still receiving emails from our boss at the Phelps Stokes Fund. He told us about the various projects that we were each supposed to spearhead moving forward, so when we were called into a board meeting in April, which concluded with our dismissal, we were completely broadsided.

Fortunately Robin, who was far savvier in those matters than I was, had fought to get a clause in our contract that included a severance package. The board was trying to make it seem as if we were being released before the April year-end mark, and thus not eligible. Fortunately, I had befriended a lawyer at John Jay College, who put me in touch with another lawyer, who wrote a letter on our behalf, stating that we had proof the work we were expected to complete extended well beyond the April year-end mark. Robin and I bonded over our mutual stand against the overly masculine board of directors, a stand for women's rights, really. We won our case, and thus was forged a timeless bond between us.

Robin is one of the most brilliant and interesting people in my life. She is a true intellectual and scholar, she is willing to go where no other person wants to go, and she is willing to stay with it until she forms that one relationship, which finally opens all the other doors. She calls herself an introvert, and I fancy myself one too, but together we have had many adventures—and some misadventures too.

We have both fought hard for the rights of other women, and for our own. She has beaten cancer, she has guided me in times of need, and she has given a voice to many of our world's invisible women. I'm so grateful that she agreed to share her story with us, and once again we met at a noisy, New York City restaurant, just like the kind we used to meet at 20 years prior. It's a perfect backdrop for Robin's busy and dynamic life, and she has chosen a Korean karaoke bar-restaurant in Williamsburg, Brooklyn. This time, with have our husbands in tow.

Robin, please tell us a little bit about how and where you grew up? What happened in your formative years that led you to becoming an anthropologist?

Robin: There were those things that family members said when I was growing up, like, when I was born, my mother said the doctor asked her which side of the family had Black blood. Then they took my father aside and asked him if we had any Arab blood. So when I heard this kind of talk later in life, it made sense that I would feel *othered*, and

I knew that would be an important thing to understand. Indeed, it has taken a lot of curiosity, intelligence, patience—and belligerence.

We also moved around a lot. My dad was with IBM, but no matter where we were, my mom used to take us to the public library. I found a series of books titled, *Fairy Tales From Other Lands*, I was about 8-years-old at the time, and I went through each book thoroughly. I couldn't believe it when I finished the last volume and that was it! It was like the end of the Earth, and I thought to myself, there must be other lands and other places, and this can't be all the stories there are to tell.

Then we moved overseas to France, which was perfect for so many reasons. Paris—say no more! I was 13 at the time, and my first plane ride was to Paris—I hadn't even been on a plane in the United States. We'd been living between New York, Virginia, and Connecticut up to that point.

Lisette: Wow, that must have been a big change for you.

Robin: It was a big deal, both geographically and class-wise, for my dad to move his family overseas—it was very prestigious. My grandfather on my mother's side had been the director of public relations for NASA, and my grandmother was in the first class of women to graduate from the Northwestern School of Journalism—they were intellectuals. What I discovered at the American School of Paris, was that I couldn't really make any American friends, so I co-opted my sister's friends.

Paris is at the intersection of governments that get overthrown, and all of those government children ended up at the American School of Paris. Lots of military kids too, so I just spotted the non-American girls, and I targeted them and made them my best friends. Turkish, Bangladeshi, Iranian…

Lisette: And they are still your best friends today?

Robin: Yes, but one of them died of leukemia. I had tried to be a bone marrow donor for her, but I wasn't a close enough match.

Lisette: Is it fair to say that living in an international city like Paris, with people from all over the world, might have planted a seed for you to get into anthropology?

Robin: Yeah, those *Fairy Tales From Other Lands* planted the first seed, and then it became embodied in all these kids I befriended in Paris from 1980-85. And our school was bombed too, by the way, and one student's father was assassinated, and one or two others had parents whose colleagues were assassinated, so it all felt very close to home.

Global politics at the time was a very real thing, and we had to say we were Canadian and not American, so it was very politicized. There were some kids I remember back in 8th grade, and this girl who sat next to me had just arrived after four days and nights on a bus from Tehran. The Shah had just been deposed in 1979, and her father was a nuclear physicist who had been detained and held back in Tehran. She and her mother were sent on a bus for safety's sake, and that's the way the world was back then. So when September 11th happened here, it was terrible of course, but I also thought, that's the real world right there, coming back to haunt us.

Lisette: Indeed, the US had become very insular prior to 9/11, and that woke us up to global politics. But one can argue that the *othering* you felt as a child was also a catalyst for your anthropological pursuits?

Robin: Well, our school offered the International Baccalaureate degree — the IB, as it's known around the world, and that gave me credit towards college. So I thought, I'm going to be an international citizen, that was the best identity I could come up with, so I just made that my identity: Robin Root, international citizen.

Barrett: OK Robin, you find yourself in this international environment in Paris, and it's a very dramatic time, obviously. I remember the Iranian revolution of 1979, which was the Iranian student's response to the American CIA, which had overthrown their democratically-elected President Mosaddegh in 1953. It took them 25 years to revolt, but they finally did. You and I are exactly the same age, so I remember this clearly, except I was growing up in rural Washington State and you were right in the middle of it, in Paris. What else happened around that time?

Robin: A couple years after the Iranian Revolution, Israel invaded southern Lebanon, and then we got this whole troupe of Lebanese kids. They were just so cool—the Lebanese are really amazing people, unflappable, and they were a perfect fit for our school.

Lisette: That was the beginning of the destruction of Beirut, formerly known as the Paris of the Middle East. OK, so you're exposed to all of this political drama in Paris, and even getting used to a sort of daily, dangerous existence.

Robin: And kind of liking it.

Lisette: Hearing other people's stories, did you gain an affinity for a deeper understanding of the people and the political situations they were fleeing from?

Robin: I did, and at one point, I went to a talk from the director of International Studies at the University of Pennsylvania. I remember sitting there and listening to her, just absorbing everything, and I was thinking, wow, there is so much more going on in Paris, than in, say, Sandy Hook, Connecticut.

Lisette: Didn't you also present an academic paper in Tehran, many years later, when you were a full professor?

Robin: Yes I did, and I want to say something about the whole Iranian thing, because I went to the University of Tehran in 2005 to present that paper. I went to the dean's house for dinner, and I remember how all the young Iranian students were so excited to return to Iran. It was the best thing that had ever happened for them, after they got rid of the Shah, who had been backed by the CIA. It was a great time for them to be home, finally.

Barrett: I bet it was, because the Shah's secret police, the Savak, were also trained by the CIA, and they committed horrendous crimes against the Iranian people. The overthrow of the Shah was the inevitable outcome of our destruction of Iranian democracy. We should have learned our lesson by now, but American politicians have very short memories.

Robin: As short as they come!

Lisette: So back at the Paris school, your world was literally being blown wide open, both with an actual bombing at your school, and the political crises that you witnessed over and over. What was it like at home, around your family?

Robin: I was up in my dad's face all the time, arguing and fighting with him, like, all the time.

Lisette: You were being put into a situation where you had to fight for your rights?

Robin: Yes, and I also learned how to understand and use silence to my advantage.

Lisette: And where did you finally go to college after you left Paris?

Robin: I got rejected from some good schools, but I did get into the University of Pennsylvania. Around the same time, a Chinese girl who I went to school with in Paris started writing to me, asking me when I would help liberate the women in China. I felt like I had done the Europe thing, and now I wanted to do Asia or Russia. This Chinese girl would write me letters from Paris and she encouraged me to learn Chinese, so I took intensive Chinese language classes at Penn.

Lisette: Did you maintain contact with her?

Robin: I did, but she ended up working for a large corporation and that's when her talk of revolution eventually disappeared from our conversations.

Lisette: So many people choose that route, and all their inspiration dies. What's interesting, however, is that your interest in Asia got you started on your academic path towards feminine liberation—at the global level.

Robin: Right, and I wrote my master's thesis on the models of womanhood during the Chinese Cultural Revolution. My IB degree from the Paris school gave me a year and half of credit at Penn, so I got both a bachelor's and master's degree at the same time in what they called, at the time, Oriental Studies. I know that Oriental is not the politically correct term now, but that's what they called it at the time.

Lisette: How much time did you spend in China all total?

Robin: Before I went to China, I had been working for the World Game Institute, which was a simulation game developed by Buckminster Fuller. Then on July 4th, 1990, just a little over a year after the Tiananmen Square Massacre in Beijing, I sent a fax to a Chinese aeronautics university, asking if they needed any English teachers. They hired me, and I ended up spending about one academic year teaching English at this Chinese aeronautics university. During my stay, I even got cast in a Kung Fu movie about a team of kick-ass Chinese policewomen! I fell in love with the Chinese language, as well as their art history.

Lisette: You were in a Kung Fu movie—that's awesome! How did you get from there to the World Game Institute, and what kind of work did you do for them?

Robin: Well, because I had lived in Europe for so many years, I had never been west of Appalachia in the United States, so I knew more about Europe than the US. After graduation from Penn, a friend and I got one of those rental car drive-away jobs, and we drove cross-country, all the way to San Francisco. Right after we arrived in San Francisco, I got a call that I had been offered this job at the World Game Institute.
It was started by Buckminster Fuller (American architect, systems theorist, and futurist), who had this theory around resource utilization. So we did these extraordinary workshops, where participants would represent a portion of a country's population and simulate all this stuff. I worked all over the US, in rural North Dakota, everywhere really. I was very moved by the whole experience, and I learned more about the US than I could have ever imagined.

Barrett: Ain't that the truth! Road trips will do that—you learn so much just from being in a new place, on the ground, hanging out with the local people. My experience touring taught me that American people are generally pretty kind and decent folks. All the stereotypes fall away.

Robin: You know, at my first or second World Game workshop, my other facilitator turned out to be a professional musician too. These were about 3-hour events, where we had to stand up, speak, and run the entire event, and then we'd ask for their evaluations at the end. That's when we'd get real, human honesty.

Lisette: That's very true, people are very different in face-to-face situations, as opposed to how they are on, say, social media. OK, so you learned a great deal about standing up and presenting information in front of regular Americans, and you got all this road experience with real people, having real human interactions.

Robin: Yes, but I also had to learn to be an extrovert, because I'm naturally an introvert. I had to tap into, and manufacture an extroverted version of my own personality, and if you're not an extrovert, it's incredibly hard to understand how difficult, and exhausting, and even painful it is to go from being an introvert to becoming an extrovert. But I learned how to do it, hard as it was.

Lisette: What was it like being back in the US, especially after all that time in Europe?

Robin: Honestly I found people to be very flat—they had flat politics, flat lives. But I eventually found my tribe, and they were the hyper-feminists. We did a protest outside of Irvine Auditorium, which used to show movies to students, but the only movie that ever made them any money was the porno flick, *Debbie Does Dallas*.

Lisette: What?!?! Penn showed a porno on campus?

Robin: Yes, and they did it repeatedly! So the feminists organized a protest, and our issue was not that we were anti-porn, but rather that our student fees were going to promote a film which was degrading to women, it was making the male students all horny, and it was making the women feel very unsafe on campus. Why would you show a porno film on our campus in the first place? I remember engaging with a particular man, in a reasonable argument, and he listened and understood. And that's when I realized that we could set up groups for men and women to get together and discuss these issues.

Lisette: So through all of this, there was an identity emerging in you—that of a heavy-duty feminist, in addition to being an international citizen.

Robin: Yeah, and I also had a Lebanese friend who gave me an Arafat scarf and I wore it everywhere.

Barrett: I have one of those too, I bought it in the Palestinian West Bank. That scarf has become the universal symbol for resistance against oppression around the world. You know, it just reminds me of all the clowns in Washington D.C. who call themselves hawks, who want to wage war on Iran, or some other Arab nation, yet none of those clowns, or very few of them, have ever served in the military, much less in actual combat.

Robin: And none of those same clowns can give birth to a child, yet they want to tell women where, when, and how they can give birth.

Barrett: There is also the universal statistic where 1-in-3 people will follow whatever dictator happens to seize power. They'll adopt hateful, oppresive policies that they rationalize with low-effort thinking, and this is why terrible men and their policies become reality. People would rather stay asleep and follow the path of least resistance—they swallow the blue pill and never wake up.

Lisette: It's also because we are cognitive misers. We apply stereotypes to people who are different, because that is easier than making the effort to figure these things out. So we see a person, or a nation, and we make a generalized assumption about them, and we often never think beyond that.

OK, how did you parlay this political and feminist awakening into getting your Ph.D. and becoming a fieldworker and an advocate for women around the world?

Robin: I had to take a natural sciences class to graduate from Penn, so I took this physical anthropology class and I absolutely fell in love with it. I thought, hey, this is the story of our species! And at Penn, there is no better place to study that—they had every artifact you ever wanted to examine. But I knew I wanted to deal with living people, and not bones and fossils, I wanted the ultimate explanation of our species, our politics, and our conflicts.

Somehow I ended up visiting a friend at the University of California, Berkeley and I found out about their medical anthropology program—perfect! I could fuse social justice with the human body and cultural variations. I knew I could get international work like that, and be able to pay my rent at the same time. I wasn't accepted into Berkeley, but I did get into UCLA, and later I did an end-run and got into Harvard as well.

Lisette: And in addition to your Ph.D. in anthropology from UCLA, you also have a master's in public health from Harvard?

Robin: Yes, and my degrees are still in their envelopes—I've never taken them out.

Barrett: Maria Williams, a Tlingit women who is in this book, also got her Ph.D. from UCLA. It's really an extraordinary school for the social sciences.

Robin: It is, and because I entered the UCLA doctoral program with a master's from Penn, I took my qualifying exams after just two years. I realized at the time that privilege happens very early on in life, because everything I did after that followed right up to where I wanted to go. To be fair, I also worked really, really hard because I wanted to do this work, but privilege was involved because my dad's job at IBM got me started at a great high school. So after about 5½ years of graduate school, I earned a second master's degree and my Ph.D.

Lisette: And where did you do your fieldwork for the Ph.D.?

Robin: In Malaysia, I knew that it would be medical-related fieldwork, which is why I needed that master's in public health from Harvard. This was in the early 1990s, right at the start of the AIDS epidemic, so I was added to a project at UCLA, specifically because the biologist in charge knew that the AIDS virus existed in the most intimate places of human interaction—and that was my realm, the realm of social science.

I finished the Harvard MPH program, and I also received a Fulbright scholarship at about the same time. Then I was told of a Chinese-Malaysian NGO, where I received a small travel grant to go to Malaysia and meet with the director of the NGO. I wanted to investigate some doctoral topics there, and I wanted to study sex workers in particular, but I knew it would be hard for a middle-class American girl like me to interview a bunch of Malaysian prostitutes and their *Johns*.

So I spent some time with a Muslim female doctor on the rural side of the island, and she gave me a Ministry of Health document that showed how they dealt with the AIDS epidemic. It described high-risk settings for HIV, which was a funny word to use—*settings*, in addition to high-risk groups like, prostitutes, fishermen, and factory workers, amongst others. I thought, wait a minute, these are factories owned by Sony and Hewlett Packard—why are they a high-risk setting for AIDS?

It turns out that there's an entirely different story about the globalization of electronics, which starts with British colonization back in the 1700s. They'd basically segregated the Malays in the rice paddies, the Chinese were working in the shops in town, and the Indians were working on the rubber plantations.

During and after the Independence of 1957, the Malaysian government kept the status quo in place. Very quickly, however, they set up these factories that required bussing in lots of Malay girls from the nice calm villages, to Chinese-dominated Penang. They also flew in plane loads of immigrant women from Indonesia and the Philippines to keep wages down. That freaked people out, and at the same time HIV was coming, so by the 1990s, all of these groups were mixing like never before. They called it *racial mixing*, so when I'd ask why factories are high risk, a lot of people would answer, "Because of the racial mixing that goes on inside," even though that had nothing to do with it. More likely it was the low wages, and some of the women had to do sex work on the side.

Lisette: Wow, that is a really dramatic atmosphere! And this is all happening where many of our electronics are made?

Robin: Exactly. I went to the factory wondering how I would talk to factory girls with the class and language differences that existed between us. I didn't know how to reach them. Then a woman reached out to me—she was going to lead a worker's strike, but if you strike in Malaysia, they just fire you on the spot. So I convinced her not to strike, and instead I said, "Let's you and me make a presentation of the worker's grievances, and then you'll go in on your own and present it." We did that, and it worked perfectly—she got their over-time reinstated, and she became a very powerful leader in the factory. I became great friends with her, and I'd visit her in her village. She became one of my liaisons to the girls in the factory.

Lisette: OK, so after you did all that fieldwork in Malaysia, you were awarded your Ph.D., and you became an anthropology professor at Baruch College, which is a very prestigious college in New York City. You went from working in Malaysia, to becoming a professor, to setting up another project in Swaziland, near South Africa. That is huge work Robin, and those are two very different continents and cultures. How do you teach your Baruch students these very complicated, international dynamics?

Robin: I wouldn't have been able to do any of that without the help and guidance of those factory girls in Malaysia. I wanted to understand how their world really worked, and Malaysia was one helluva education in itself! That's actually how I came to work for the Phelps Stokes Fund in the first place, where I met Lisette, but I also had to figure out what I was going to do next. I had this opportunity to go to Cape Town and Johannesburg in South Africa, to attend a conference with Charles Ogletree of Harvard Law School. He was going there to present an award to Nelson Mandela and Bill Clinton.

Lisette: This is when your study of AIDS took you to Swaziland, correct?

Robin: Right, I had met a missionary on one of those flights to South Africa, who was doing amazing work in Swaziland around the same time that I was offered the professorship at Baruch College in Manhattan. In fact, I got the invitation for the Baruch job interview the day before I headed to the Cape Town AIDS conference. Forty-eight hours after I got back, I gave my talk, and that night I was offered the position at Baruch. As an aside, on my way to the Baruch interview, a bird totally shat all over the left shoulder of my lavender silk blazer. A woman on the subway alerted me to it, so I scrambled to wash it off before meeting the dean. Ever tried to wash silk quickly—you can't!

Lisette: I remember that I met up with you right as you were headed to that interview, and I said it was a good omen! Italians believe that if a bird shits on you, it's good luck—I expect it's simply to make one feel better on such an occasion. You know Robin, there's a pattern emerging here where you get offered these amazing opportunities, right at the moment when you are about to start the next adventure in your life.

Robin: Ultimately, I owe my tenure at Baruch to the factory girls in Malaysia, and the HIV/AIDS caregivers in Swaziland. They taught me so much about being human in the worst kind of devastation. What those caregivers are battling is a disease that is inside of them, inside of their loved ones, so it's a different kind of fear, and a different kind of love they have to show each other. And it's a completely different kind of love, because it's so hard to take care of someone with HIV, so the love is coming from a very deep place. It's really, really hard work, and it requires a certain kind of generosity of heart—it's what makes a person more human than the person next to them. It's getting through the next day, and what will keep them all happy.

I've been working in Swaziland since 2005, and I have hundreds of pages of field notes. God, they really shared a lot with me. I think my real power in all of this, is collecting stories and fairytales from other lands, except that my stories are about sicknesses, suffering, and death in other places. And I'm good at that.

Barrett: Someday you are going to write an incredible book Robin, like those old European fairy tales, which are usually about sickness, untimely death, and darkness across the land. Except your book will show how all those terrible things are the way a person, or a nation, finds their redemption.

Lisette: Robin, you've spent more time in Malaysia and Swaziland than anywhere else in the world, aside from New York City. How do you take those people's Indigenous wisdom and pass it on in the classroom?

Robin: Mostly I teach my students about my mistakes—and I have plenty of them. My students love hearing about my mistakes, but they also love hearing about the supernatural world. The supernatural world is very present in Malaysia and Swaziland, especially with babies and young children, and they love those stories.

Lisette: And how did your personal struggle fighting breast cancer help you to understand what these women have gone through? Did it help you to empathize with them more closely?

Robin: I had access to great healthcare, so there's no way my suffering can compare to what those girls went through—still go through. When they heard I had breast cancer, they gave me a high five—it was like we were partners in crime. Here's another example: in Swaziland, near the end of my stay, I was trying to get through my interviews quickly—I had so many to do! I still had several villages to go to, and then I met this Swazi woman who also had breast cancer. I asked her to tell me what happened to her, and she said that this other woman told her she would die within a year, which really pissed me off. I said really, is that what she said? Then I lifted up my shirt, I showed her my mastectomy scar and I said, "You're not going to die, you're going to live a very long time, just like I am."

Lisette: You've always been a fighter Robin, always. Was there a point at which you felt like you didn't need to be so tough, or did it perhaps make you even tougher?

Robin: I think it happened when I started teaching. I currently teach *Sociology of Health and Illness, Qualitative Research Methods,* and *Introduction To Cultural Anthropology.* I would say my classes are 50/50 men and women and they are mostly people of color, so they totally do not fit the modern census form. They never knew how to fill out those damn forms anyway. One of my students told me recently that she was no longer afraid to speak out, but it's tricky, especially for girls who are at a lower income level, or when English is not their first language. I tell them to create a social network right away, because studies have shown that you will live longer with a social network, even if you're an introvert like me. You have to create that extrovert personality and go out and make friends.

Lisette: That's an incredible story Robin, and all your work is about women telling you their gritty truths, but somehow they pull through and survive, even finding happiness along the way.

Robin: But the other side of the story is that women can also undermine each other, when they say things like, "You're going to die from cancer," or when they vote against the best interests of all women.

It's a big taboo in the sisterhood to undermine each other, so I'm like, hey, let's find the women who undermine us, and let's call them out.

Dr. Maria Williams

Tlingit Musicologist & Professor Of Native Studies

"We do not inherit the earth from our ancestors, we borrow it from our children."

-Tlingit Proverb

Lisette: Maria Williams was Barrett's undergraduate and graduate advisor at the University Of New Mexico. She has had a profound and ongoing influence on his work with Indigenous people in the Peruvian Amazon, the Alaskan Arctic, and beyond. Barrett, I can't thank enough for introducing me to this amazing woman, so can you please do the honors for our readers?

Barrett: When I was a student at the University Of New Mexico in the early 2000s, my focus of study was anthropology, linguistics, human rights, and ethnomusicology. The latter discipline is a form of musicology that encompasses all of the others, by looking at world music as a focusing lens for culture. Much of my time at UNM was spent studying these diverse subjects with Dr. Maria Williams. Her engaging classes seemed to encompass all of those fields—culture, identity, language (especially Indigenous languages), human rights, sacred ceremonies, and of course music from around the world. Her incredible methodology taught us how to look at cultures around the world with the highest levels of scholarship and wisdom.

Years later, when I became a music professor myself, I would often write to Dr. Williams to ask her advice on syllabuses I was writing, classes I was teaching, and to invite myself up to Alaska to visit and get some teaching experience in her classroom. Dr. Williams was also my field advisor when I worked on that project with the Shipibo Shamans in the Peruvian Amazon, and she introduced me to the Gwich'in people in the Arctic National Wildlife Refuge, where I worked on a similar project for that tribe. Both of those experiences were huge, eye-opening, revelations into how Indigenous people are dealing with the climate crisis, and the devastating effects of the fossil fuel industry in the delicate habitats of the Amazon Rainforest and the Alaskan Arctic.

Lisette and I flew to Alaska to speak with Dr. Williams about her remarkable teaching style, because she was, and is, the greatest scholar-academic I have ever had the privilege of studying with, at any level of education. Her style of teaching is so powerful that anyone who takes one of her classes, even if they didn't have a formal music education, would leave her class with a vast knowledge of global culture, and a deep sense that all of it was inextricably connected. Her ability to convey the sacred power of Indigenous ceremonies in particular, is unique in academia.

For example, Maria could explain how the Native American songs of Southern California were a way for the people to understand the migration patterns of the birds, which followed the seasonal changes. Or how Amazonian shamans can actually envision their healing songs in their mind's eye, before they actually sing the songs out loud. Or how the traditional Pow Wow dance is really one of the earliest forms of what we now call a rave or dance party. Or how an Indian *raga* or an Arabic *maqam* might be played at certain times of the day for a specific ritual, or to display a certain kind of feeling. All of her classes are, to put it succinctly, absolutely fascinating.

Lisette: We wanted to ask Dr. Williams what qualities make a great teacher in the 21st century, and why she does this for so many lucky students? In addition to that, how does a Native American woman with a Ph.D. (who also happens to play a damn good fiddle) pass on her own Tlingit wisdom to her students, Indigenous and non-Indigenous alike?

It's a chilly November, but we're in Maria's cozy, warm home in Anchorage, where she has cooked a salmon dinner for us, and her lovely sister Gloria is joining us as well.

Maria, would you please tell us how you first discovered music up here in Alaska, and what made you want to study it as an academic pursuit?

Maria: I just loved music when I was growing up in Anchorage, and I played in the school band, trying out clarinet, violin, and viola. Western classical music was really all there was up here back then, but then as an undergraduate in college, I heard all of the Alaskan Native music and I just totally fell in love with it. But the opportunity to study it didn't exist yet, so Western music was all I had when I studied at Dominican University in San Rafael, just north of San Francisco.

There, I heard the great Lebanese singer, Fairuz, and I fell in love with Middle Eastern music too. I started buying all the world music albums from the Nonesuch label: Balinese music, Arabic music, Brazilian music, and all the other exotic forms of music. I also taught private music lessons for about 5 years, until around the age of 27, when I applied to UCLA for graduate school. I didn't get in there on my first attempt, but I did on the second! I was about 28 when I started graduate school in ethnomusicology, and I played in a variety of music ensembles at UCLA.

I just loved the diversity of musicians, and I was inspired by all the different nationalities. UCLA had all these performing ensembles, where we learned all the different styles of music that were not built around Western musical pedagogy. And I also studied with the great Arabic music scholar, A.J. Racy, and he taught me how to look at the world much differently.

Lisette: What a great atmosphere to be immersed in, to get to study all that different music. What kind of music did you focus on for your master's and Ph.D. research?

Maria: I did my masters thesis on Tlingit music, which is the music of my people, the Indigenous people of coastal Alaska. And then I did my Ph.D. research on even more Alaskan Native music. Then I came back to Alaska after I had finished everything except writing my dissertation. I got a position at the Institute of American Indian Arts, however, after only two years, they lost most of their funding and laid off most of the faculty, including me. I had just started dating a Native artist from Jemez Pueblo in New Mexico, so I moved to Jemez where I could finish my dissertation.

I set up a little office in his art studio—it only had a little wood stove, and I had to buy an extension cord to power my computer, and that's where I started writing my dissertation. I was writing about the renaissance of Alaskan song and dance, something that was just starting to happen right as I was working on my dissertation.

Lisette: I was introduced to that style of music and dance on this trip and it's so beautiful and powerful! It's truly unique in the world, and the drumming and singing is just incredible. Were Native people not interested in their music and culture prior to this renaissance?

Maria: Well, when I was growing up, this kind of Indigenous dancing was seen as suspect, and there was a lot of racism around it. It wasn't cool to wear that kind of Native clothing or regalia, much less dance to Native music while wearing it.

But then during the Land Claims Settlement of 1971, there was a political movement that united all the Alaska Native peoples to fight for their lands, and at a number of their political gatherings, dancing became publicly celebrated. Their major political organization, the Alaska Federation of Natives (AFN), was started in about 1966 and that helped push through the Land Rights Act of 1971. That's when AFN started having these dance nights, known as Quyana Nights. Other major dance festivals arose in the late 1970s and 1980s, and now dancing and music is everywhere in Alaska.

Barrett: Yep, that's what I remember the very first time I came here in 2006—the music and dance was everywhere, and it was powerful.

Lisette: Why was Native dancing repressed in the first place, was it political or religious oppression?

Maria: Mostly it came from Evangelical missionaries who said it was the devil, and they really tried to prevent any of the old ceremonies or anything else that was shamanic or animistic. And there was a lot of disease, like the tuberculosis epidemic that killed many people and made many more sick. The various Christian denominations were dividing up all of Alaska, and I found the actual document of their meeting in the Sheldon Jackson Archive, in Sitka, Alaska. It was a 1974 Presbyterian home board meeting, held in New York City, where all the Christian denominations met and decided how they were going to divide up Alaska—without any Native people being present, mind you!

Lisette: That is just awful, but that's the story of missionization around the world, especially in North and South America. The churches just did whatever they wanted to do, without even consulting the Indigenous elders. They destroyed their cultures, their beliefs, and oppressed them. What happened after you found that damning document in Sitka?

Maria: That was a big piece of my dissertation, which showed how the dances and ceremonies had been deliberately repressed by the Evangelical missionaries. When I finally earned my Ph.D. in 1996, I was offered a postdoctoral fellowship with the Ford Foundation, where I studied the surviving ceremonial dances of Alaska. After that was over, I realized that I wanted a teaching job, so on somewhat of a slim chance, I applied at the University of New Mexico. I made one phone call, and one call only—to the office of the only dean I happened to know there. For whatever reason, by chance or divine intervention, he happened to answer the phone himself—it was not his secretary.

He hired me right then and there, over the phone, and my salary was $33,000. This was back in 1999 so it wasn't much, but they gave me a lot of creative space, and they allowed me to start the first Native American music class at UNM. I taught there from 1999-2011, so I really cut my teeth as a professor there. That was when I realized that I really loved teaching, creating curriculums, and bringing Indigenous music into the student's awareness.

Barrett: It was around 2004 when I started taking classes from you, and it was that summer when I went to the Peruvian Amazon to do my fieldwork with the Shipibo. You gave me the best advice for that, because I have to admit, I was a little scared to go all the way to the Amazon and work with people I had never met before. You just said, "Have a good time, do the best work you can, and the people will love you." And you were exactly right, thank you for preparing me for that Maria, I literally couldn't have done it without you.

Maria: Oh stop it....(everyone laughs)

Lisette: Maria, how did you end up coming back to Alaska to become the Director of Alaska Native Studies at the University of Alaska? I mean, that is a really big department to oversee—the responsibilities must be huge!

Maria: It was 2011 when I was offered the position of Director Of Alaska Native Studies, and I was just compelled to take the job. I also had a desire to come home and help the youngest generation of students, because there is a real struggle between Indigenous versus Western education, as well as a need for more Indigenous curriculum in general.

One of the first projects I oversaw, was following around this famous basket weaver. I filmed her on a long journey across Alaska, as she gathered the tender birch roots in the limited window of opportunity she had to gather them. I received a grant to fund the expedition, and I followed her with a video camera to all the villages she visited along the Yukon River.

I saw, firsthand, how smart and resourceful the Native kids were, and how they could fix almost anything—even engines, despite the fact they had no stores, and they had to figure out how to fix or create anything they needed. These were healthy and culturally rich communities, but the school system had devalued them. Having Native teachers, however, changes all that.

You know, my father was sent to one of those horrible missionary boarding schools, where he was punished for even speaking his own Native language, Tlingit, and this was when 90% of Alaskan Natives were sick with tuberculosis!

Barrett: Your dad was Tlingit, and I seem to remember that your mom was from a different tribe? I became friends with her in 2006, when I came to Anchorage and stayed with you. Your mom and I were both recovering from our mutual knee and ankle surgeries, so we compared our scars. (everyone laughs)

Maria: Yeah, my mother was raised in Indiana and she was Blackfoot, but her family did not raise her with the Native ways. She ended up in Alaska because of that tuberculosis epidemic—she was a nurse that got sent up here, and she met my father in the hospital. They fell in love, got married, and had five kids.

Lisette: That is a beautiful love story!

Maria: It was, and it was all because of that tuberculosis epidemic. The Native people were sent to these sanitariums in Alaska and also, oddly enough, New Mexico. The doctors would target those communities until they eradicated the disease.

My father came from a family of nine brothers and sisters, and he worked with me when I was doing my master's fieldwork on Tlingit music back in the 1980s. He really loved it, because he was getting to speak his old language again, and learn the traditional songs. And when we would go to a potlatch, which is like a big party where food and gifts are given to the visitors, they didn't want to let us go! You see the Tlingit are matriarchal, and the women own the land titles and the names, so there is a huge family support network when someone is visiting. It is especially strong if someone is sick, and then everything is taken care of. It's really beautiful how much the communities take care of one another.

Lisette: It's terrible to think how much of that we have lost in our own American culture. We don't even know how to take care of our sick people anymore, and the elderly and the homeless are just kicked to the curb. We have lost whatever wisdom they may have had, squandered it on consumerism.

Maria: Not in Native, Indigenous culture—we honor the elderly for their wisdom. We also have the moiety system (a French word for societal halves) so my mother was from the beaver clan, which is under the raven moiety. My dad was from the killer whale clan, which is under the eagle moiety. It was beautiful to watch how these clans worked together, and how they took care of each other.

When I was a youth in Anchorage, school was really hard, and we were not acknowledged or accepted as Native at school. We were too far away from our extended Tlingit family, and my father wouldn't teach the Tlingit language because he remembered being punished for it at the boarding school. So I took Tlingit language classes at the University Of Alaska, and now there is a full-on, Native language renaissance happening there. The classes are full of both young and older students, these are highly sophisticated classes, and the people are inspired to learn their original languages. Cultural identity through Native languages is a big resonator with young people now, just like Native music and dance, which is making a big comeback, largely driven by the youth. Everything is driven by young people, just like it was with the dancing, when it first started to make its comeback in the 1970s.

Barrett: I remember you teaching us about Native American languages, the sophistication of the verb categories, and how the young people of every generation reinvent their language. Which is also why languages continue to evolve—the youth are the drivers of change, and they create the new identity through their languages.

Maria: That's right, and another thing, which is very important with Native languages, is that they are gender neutral. They have highly sophisticated kinship terms, and they are far more evolved in their verb categories than Latin-based, European languages. All of this interest in Native culture is a push back against capitalism—it's a reidentification of Indigenous identity. Young people are very empowered right now, and these kids want the ability to speak, sing, and dance their Native culture.

Lisette: Maria, how, or rather when, did you start to feel like you were coming into your personal power? Like, when did you really feel like you were becoming an empowered, Native American woman and teacher?

Maria: Empowerment started to come when I worked with the King Island Inupiaq community, who are originally from the Seward Peninsula. With them, I really started to see the power of Indigenous music and its connection to shamanism. The King Island drumming is so powerful, and they see the top of their drum as being the frame on the underside of the drum. It's an inversion of what we normally think of as the head of the drum. This is also why they call their drum, *The Future Eye*—because of its shamanic power. Growing up around Native shamanism creates a kind of magical realism, which the missionaries attempted to stamp out, but it still survives to this day, because it was so instilled in the Native peoples.

We would tell shamanic stories back and forth as kids, but we could not share those stories in a Western classroom, because people wouldn't believe them. Yet between the Native students, the stories were totally believable.

I also really felt that power when I was living in New Mexico at Jemez Pueblo, because it was there that I experienced the old teachings. The Pueblo and Navajo languages, and their ceremonies, are still very intact, because the New Mexico Pueblos were far more resilient than the other tribes. They went to war with the Spanish conquistadors, and the Native students at the University Of New Mexico became radicalized, because of the history of violence by the Spanish. The Alaskan Natives, however, were much more damaged by disease and colonial capitalism, which is why their cultures suffered so much.

Barrett: Yeah, the Pueblo communities have some really incredible dances, which I was able to see when I was a student down there.

Maria: You know, the single most powerful ceremony I have ever experienced, was the death ceremony for a woman from Jemez Pueblo. The medicine society members were singing her spirit away with the most incredible polyphonic singing I have ever heard. It was absolutely stunning, and I have never heard anything like it anywhere, before or since. It was so powerful to hear that, and I had to ask myself the question—where did all of our Alaskan ceremonies go?

Lisette: I can only imagine what that must have sounded like. I've heard polyphonic singing in the Amazon Rainforest by the Shipibo Shamans, and it was utterly mesmerizing.

Maria: We have to remember these things, because it's so important for Indigenous culture! I really believe that education is the key, so when I teach undergraduates, 50% of them are Indigenous kids. They are learning to value their worldview, the meanings of their words and languages, the importance of their names, and the sacredness of hunting as a subsistence lifestyle. They are learning how the tribe's collective consciousness works, and even though the elders still run the show, it's very subtle, and they can feel it.

Lisette: How do you transmit this kind of deep understanding now, as a professor? How do you pass on this wisdom to your students?

Maria: Well, I really love teaching, and I put an emphasis on their writing, which helps them to evolve their own voice. You know, education is really a healing modality, and it totally healed me. I really believe this, so I want my students to be empowered to question capitalism and imperialism, and this terribly destructive corporate world we are currently living in. We already know how it is destroying our planet, but this next generation has to decide what we are going to do about it.

Lisette: Gloria, what do you think of all this? Was your experience similar to your sister, Maria?

Gloria: Well of course, we grew up together! And now I'm the one who writes the official birth certificates at the hospital, so I give the official names for all these new human beings entering the world. Unfortunately, I have seen an increase in alcoholism and opioid addiction amongst Indigenous mothers. The paradox is that Indigenous mothers are incredibly nurturing and often the best mothers of any demographic. But the loss of language and ceremony has left a hole in our people, which is exacerbated by colonialism and capitalism.

You know, the mark of a healthy society is the one that takes care of its people, that hunts and grows food together, that looks after one another. Native people have a natural talent for creating things and trading them with other people, but this is not the same thing as capitalism. I just don't believe in capitalism, because it just doesn't work in the long term—it only destroys. However, I do believe socialism could help everyone.

Barrett: I feel the same way, because Lisette and I own a small business—a media company really, that creates albums of music, books of stories, and we're just starting to do videos and films. We sell these creations directly to people, and hopefully it educates and enlightens them, at the same time as being interesting and entertaining.

Lisette: Right, and this is not the same thing as extractive capitalism. We're just a small business, creating books and albums and then selling them to people. It is not unlike what Indigenous people naturally do, which is to create beautiful things to sell or trade. Both of these systems are holistic and sustainable, and are not the same thing as exploiting people's labor for a low wage, or stealing their natural resources from public lands, which is what modern capitalism does. It's fascinating how our definitions and choice of words creates our reality.

Maria: It's also interesting that the etymology for the word *professor* means, *someone who professes knowledge*. I profess that knowledge is power, knowledge is transformation, and knowledge can help us save the planet. Education is, ultimately, a political act.

Lisette: Right on Maria! Yes, teaching is definitely a political act, and all three of us are current or former professors of different subjects, so we know this directly. We teach our knowledge to the students, and thus they become empowered. The evidence of teaching as a political act is in the fact that far right factions would try to suppress education, who try to defund it, and who want to make it where only the wealthy and privileged can have a good education.

Maria: Western classrooms are just terrible—everybody is in a row, why not in a circle? In my classes, you can bring food, you can bring your dog, you can bring your parents—everyone is welcome in my classroom. Bring whomever you want, it's all about learning, together.

One of the things I am working on right now, is how to redesign a new classroom space, with a completely new configuration. Every human being has a different shape, size, and height. You can't just have a universal desk or a universal chair, because it's difficult to learn when you are uncomfortable.

Lisette: Maria, can you please talk a little more about the power of shamanism, because in all of the women we have interviewed, there is this underlying theme of a magical, mysterious, unseen world that has been suppressed by the patriarchy, but the women can still see it. This seems intuitive for Indigenous people, but even with some of the other Healers, Teachers, and Artists we have interviewed, they all talked about feeling guided and even witnessing spiritual events that opened a new doorway in their lives. It's very much the realm of new worlds, new ideas, and new possibilities.

A shaman is someone who works between those worlds, so I want to ask you, as a highly respected Indigenous professor, how do you occupy the role between the Indigenous and the modern world? You've stated that your life mission is to educate and empower students, so how do you bring real power back into education, where *The Mystery* is respected? Can you please give us your take on the role of the Indigenous teacher as a kind of *world teacher*?

Maria: My vision is to bring balance back to the health of the people, the Earth, the oceans, the atmosphere, and to address the loss of species on the planet. The problem is the global media, which is corporate-controlled and owned by big business, whose interest is in keeping these truths away from the public. These things should be front and center headlines, and if they were, I think people would behave much differently if they knew what was happening.

When I bring up the global climate crisis in class, people seem disconnected from it. You know, in reality the planet will survive, but humans may not. Corporate farming and the evil way they treat animals, the trillions spent on weapons to kill people of other religions, when we could, instead, actually cure cancer, stop global hunger, and fix so many other things that would turn the planet around. But the powers that be won't allow that—it's not in their financial interests to do so.

Lisette: I know, like, why are we still dependent on fossil fuels at this point in human history? It has been proven over and over again, that fossil fuel kills the environment, kills animals, and kills people, yet the oil corporations still want to drill for more oil and destroy the last pristine wildernesses on Earth, like here in the Arctic National Wildlife Refuge. What could they possibly be thinking—or rather, not-thinking?

Maria: The K-12 education system does not teach students to think or question. It's all about memorization and indoctrination, and it doesn't really change until college and graduate school, when real critical thinking begins.

In the 1960s, the hippies went to school and that really scared the corporate establishment. It scared the oligarchs and the power brokers, and that's why they changed education to be this watered down nonsense, because they saw that it radicalized people into action. Education is becoming so expensive that only the wealthy are benefitting from it, and even with a college education, you're still part of the wage-slave system—it's designed to turn you into that.

My entire purpose as a teacher is to empower young people, so that they are in control of their destinies, to be able to make informed decisions about their lives, and to take the necessary action to change the direction of their planet.

And I won't be stopped from doing that.

The Reverend Yuko Conniff

Retired Physician & Zen Teacher

"You are the sky. Everything else is just the weather."
– Pema Chodron

Lisette: Barrett and I have both practiced Buddhism for almost 25 years now—I studied the Tibetan style, and he studied Japanese Soto Zen. For him, it started in 1997 at the Detroit Street Zen Center in Los Angeles, where he began his studies with the Reverend Yuko Conniff. Barrett, can you please describe for us how your Zen training began with Yuko, and how that training has influenced your spiritual life?

Barrett: I've studied with Yuko since the mid 1990s, and through her disciplined method and superb guidance, I learned the spiritual tenets of Zen meditation, as well as other forms of mindfulness or *Everyday Zen*, as we call it. These practices help to clear up the tangled, conceptual mind, so that we can enter into a state of deep awareness in everything we do.

Lisette understands this too, because of her spiritual practice through the Dalai Lama's lineage of Tibetan Buddhism. She even completed 4 years of silent meditation retreat, and is considered a *Lama*, a teacher of *The Way*. Yet both of us continue to learn as much as we can from other teachers, even as we teach our own students. One of those ongoing relationships is with Yuko, where we do a regular *Dokusan* (private study) with her. Nowadays, and because of the physical distance between the Pacific Northwest and California, we use computer technology to communicate with her at her Zendo in Los Angeles, California.

Lisette: For this particular interview, we routed our flight through Los Angeles on our way home from the Peruvian Amazon, where we had just interviewed the Shipibo. We wanted to speak with Yuko in her traditional Zendo, a place where Barrett spent several years studying. This is a great honor, because studying with a spiritual teacher is one thing, whereas interviewing them about their personal story is a very different kind of learning.

We are sitting on black cushions, known as *zafus*, in the main mediation room of the Detroit Street Zen Center, which is one block off the Miracle Mile stretch of Wilshire Boulevard, a street that epitomized the golden age of Hollywood in the 1920s, 30s, and 40s. Now, the Miracle Mile is full of modern apartment buildings, museums, and retail shops, the homogenizing effects that we've seen across every Western city. But inside Yuko's airy, sunlit Zendo, there is a different kind of atmosphere altogether. The walls are painted white, and the room is nearly bare except for the large wooden Buddha on the altar, a Zen painting that Barrett created, which hangs above the entrance, and several more black zafus that the students use to meditate upon. There are fresh flowers on the altar, as well as some sandalwood incense that is wafting in the air.

After having some tea and an informal conversation to catch up on the three years since Barrett last visited, we jump right in with our conversation—it has a strong political bent. I really enjoy when spiritual teachers are politically engaged.

Barrett: Yuko, it's so great to see you again, and for you to finally meet Lisette in person. It's wonderful to be back here in the Zendo, but what a strange and dangerous time we seem to be living in. It's like everything you taught us about *Karma* and the law of cause and effect is actually playing out inside our country. We are being divided by ongoing political, environmental, and economic crises, we have these awful, white supremacists in power, and they have fostered a real hatred towards immigrants, and Mexican people in particular. This resulted in the mass shooting at the Walmart in El Paso, Texas, where my mother-in-law's good friend was killed.

These hateful men have actually put immigrant children in cages at the Mexican border, and they rationalize it under a twisted philosophy that makes absolutely no sense to anyone with the most basic moral principles. Lisette's parents are Mexican immigrants, and she is an American citizen who grew up in El Paso, so she has seen and experienced this kind of racism directly. How did these extremely conservative, White men totally lose their morality, or any semblance of human decency?

Yuko: We did something to allow this to happen—it didn't just happen out of the blue. The people I see who are fervently supporting these views have, what in Buddhism we would call, the *animal realm viewpoint*, or a way of viewing things where they see things in a narrow, blinders-on kind of way. There is no depth or looking deeper at the issues—they just don't think very deeply about anything.

You can be uneducated and poor and still have, what I call, street wisdom, or life wisdom, which I see a lot with the Latino population here. But people with the narrow viewpoint don't have that wisdom. So you ask the question, why do they not have wisdom? If you look at the Latino folks here, they have this incredible sense of family and wisdom when you talk with them, and there is something in their eyes that knows about life. However, the folks who don't look deeply are usually asking, "What's in it for me?" Something's lacking there.

Lisette: And this is the heart of what we've been discovering on this journey, which is defining what feminine power is. From a Buddhist perspective, the female is the embodiment of wisdom, but the pendulum has shifted to such a male-dominated world, and not just the physical male, but also the energetic male. So what does it take to swing the pendulum back, and how do we help that process along, how do we help people along, and how do we maintain the balance?

Yuko: It's all about dialogue, so we have to get to know each other again. It's a huge country, with many different ethnic groups, and different geography. I spent 12 years in a monastery in a town with 650 people, near the Iowa border. They were farmers and we had to be able to talk with them and see where they were coming from. They were organically tied in with the weather and the Earth, which was beautiful, and they were very slow in how they lived their lives. They thought we were crazy because we were so fast-paced, but it was through dialogue and living next to them that, over the years, we developed a tremendous rapport.

Barrett: That's very true, the Midwest and the South have a slower pace and they are more conservative, but there are also many great people in those states. So much classic American literature and music came out of the South: Mark Twain, William Faulkner, Maya Angelou, Alice Walker, Joy Harjo—many of the greatest writers and poets came from those places and they created some of the most progressive forms of literature and music that people all over the world love. Now it seems like the Internet and social media is the place where this disconnect between Americans has really entrenched, and even weaponized itself.

Yuko: I think we've become disassociated from things because of technology, but it's a double-edged sword. We can communicate better with each other, with people in other countries, and we can communicate better in terms of just straight-talking to each other. But people on their cell phones—they're in a kind of cocoon, so when they're on their phone, they can communicate with that one person, but they become cut off from their environment, the sun, the flowers, or saying hello to somebody on the street. I think that's what technology has done—it's really dissociated us from the whole, it's made us much more individualistic and egoistic in that way.

I mean look at selfies. It seems absurd, this idea of putting a picture of yourself out into the world, as opposed to celebrating the people who are with you, or the scenery. I really feel this disassociation from technology, in terms of that bubble. I tutor kids, and they can really get into their computers, to the point where they don't know how to relate to daily life, so it's taking us away from our environment. It looks like it's connecting us, and it is, but it's doing it in a way that's not healthy—and were not using it in the right way.

We really have to learn how to grow up with our technology, we have to be able to do that. I always ask people who I see on the street,

"Do you ever leave your cell phone at home?" Invariably the answer is "No," people rarely leave them at home.

Lisette: We see this at the beach near our house—people are always on their cell phones, including couples who stare at their phones, as they walk side by side. They miss the beautiful sunset taking place right in front of them, totally oblivious to their environment.

Yuko: The interesting thing is, I take a walk every single day, and a lot of people have dogs here, and the people who walk their dogs do not have their cell phones! 95% of them don't have their phones out. They are paying attention to their dog's life.

Lisette: I've seen mothers with baby strollers pay more attention to their phones than they do to their children, which is another problem entirely! I think it's somewhat of a generational thing too. Millennials are really into their technology and social media—they were the first generation to grow up with computers. What do you think about the younger generations? What can they do to remedy the current political and environmental crisis, to bring balance back into our national dialogue?

Yuko: Not very many young people come to learn about Zen anymore. Most of my interactions are teaching my students via Skype, since many have moved away from Los Angeles, or sometimes it's from just going out in the world, like shopping or doing errands. Not many come here though, because within a five mile radius there are probably six other Zendos. Zen centers are all over West Hollywood and greater Los Angeles now—they're everywhere. But the whole world is your spiritual practice, so I meet Millennials wherever I go, and I have great discussions with them—I get a pretty good feeling from them. Some are not that interested in what is going on, but a lot of them are.

My generation, which is a bit older than your generation, grew up during the Vietnam War, so we dealt with some pretty pithy issues. My friends were going off to fight in Vietnam—everything was very real. Every day was like, wow, what's going to happen next? There were protests, the country was being torn apart over the war, and then Martin Luther King and Bobby Kennedy were assassinated, all in one year.

There was that horrible thing at the 1968 Chicago convention, where the police brutally beat up the protesting students. We were much more self-introspective, and there were deeper issues for us. That's why Zen took hold, along with all the experimenting with LSD and other psychedelics, which was all about looking inwardly for self-realization.

The kids today don't have that kind of war hanging over their heads, but they do in a different way, because we still have domestic terrorism, a collapsing economy, mass shootings, and the world is changing so rapidly. The one thing I've seen is a slight difference in their intensity, because they haven't experienced impermanence the way we did, so life is a little more cushy for them. Maybe it's just that age, but with commitment, some of them will become very engaged.

I was in the first Women's March and we had 750,000 people at that march, it was incredible. And I went to the second Women's March, and then the Gun March. At the Gun March, the young people really mobilized because it had a lot to do with them—they were the speakers and they organized it. There were probably 150,000 people in attendance and they were very motivated, but I don't know if they can sustain it. They have to balance their life with their studies and getting into college, but they are starting to understand about impermanence, because gun violence can end your life instantly. All of them told me, I cannot wait till I can vote! Over the next few years, over five million young people will be of voting age, and I can tell you, not a single person there was going to vote for anyone associated with the NRA or any of the vehement gun rights advocates.

Lisette: Yeah, the tables have definitely turned on the NRA, that's for sure. The Millennials and Generation Z are going to be a huge political force, if they choose to become active. They are the most educated and progressive generation in American history, perhaps in all of the world, so if they don't become active, it's really at their own peril. They are, however, very good at using social media as a mobilizing tool, and maybe that's where they are most effective—mobilizing their generation to take action.

Yuko: Another thing about technology is that it, and social media are creating a shorter attention span in people. When you read a book, you have to sit and turn the pages—it takes time! These kids are not accustomed to that, they want everything fast, and they like the idea that they can have everything, now. As a consequence, they don't know how to focus, so it's an incredible and transforming age, and incredible things are happening. But the danger is that we can destroy our ability to see the truth by distorting things so much.

The Internet is distorting our ability to see facts as they are, which is ultimate to the practice. Google gives you what you want, when you search for it, but it's not objective—it's designed to cater to your particular, individual taste or viewpoint. But that's a false reality, and it's distorting our ability to see the facts as they are. This is ultimate to any spiritual practice, and that's the biggest danger right now—the convoluting and distorting of facts to become what you want them to be, rather than what they really are. That is the real danger for the future.

Lisette: From your perspective, what is the remedy for this, for finding truth again?

Yuko: There is a very deep distrust of the government, of scientific facts, and a lack of education because of this twisting of truth. I think education, and an effort to understand each other is very necessary to deal with this problem.

Barrett: I remember back in the 1990s when I studied here at the Zen center, and you used to say to us, "Don't take my word for it—see if it's true within your own experience, use the empirical method." Unfortuntely, most people don't do that, they just do whatever is in their personal interest, or whatever political faction they happen believe in. They've lost the ability for critical thinking.

Yuko: I think that kind of deep questioning really scares people, because when you don't question things, you feel more secure.

Lisette: In psychology, the research I did on stereotypes and racism and the stories we create, found evidence for the fact that we tend to to be very simplistic in our extrapolations. We choose to make quick decisions and judgments about people and situations, without any desire to question our own thought process. That's what we need to find out—why are we lazy, and why do we desire to oversimplify complex thought processes?

Yuko: That is my point, and what seems evident here, is that there is something inherently wrong with why we are allowing that to happen. We have to look at some of the deeper issues of what's on TV, reality shows, and the fact that our society does not revere wisdom anymore. It reveres celebrity, it reveres fame, but this is a very superficial, self-centered approach that doesn't want to look at the deeper issues. That's what we have to look at, but we're just not there yet. We've just started talking to each other, but this current American culture doesn't revere wisdom, and it's very strange. We just had a very wise leader, President Obama, and I believe that was a bit threatening to some people.

Barrett: And there is also a lot of extreme religious rhetoric that has become dominant in the national conversation. This is not good for the nation or the world, which is why the Founders separated church and state in the Constitution. I would hope that the vast majority of people will continue to pursue science, but even then, we are choosing not to value wisdom in the same way. Science by itself is not wisdom, as is evidenced in the way we have misused it—like continuing to make atomic bombs and other weapons of mass destruction.

Yuko: You have to look at the real things that are causing this though. I worked with a lot of Latino folks, whom I love, and they have real wisdom. They had something they understood about life, a deeper understanding, a kind of humility and appreciation for what they had. But a segment of our population has no reverence for that at all, and that's the real problem. Now we're into celebrity and materialism.

Barrett: I also think it comes down to the problems in late-stage capitalism, which is like late-stage cancer, and this gets to the core of this book, and the interviews we've been conducting. Because when you look around the world at the really old cultures, like the Indigenous cultures, it's usually the women who carry the wisdom. Most of those cultures are tens of thousands of years old, they are matriarchal, and their wisdom has been passed on through countless generations. But this male-dominated global economy, which is built on exploiting labor, natural resources, and selling plastic crap is, quite literally, killing the planet. When that becomes the priority instead of the preservation of the Earth, then we are really in dire straits.

Lisette: Maybe this cultural laziness comes from things being too easy. Like my mom and my aunts who came from Mexico—they knew what real poverty was like. Finding food in a grocery store, or clothing at a mall, allows you to work a job and live your life differently. Many Latino people join the American military too, because they value service to our country. Coming from real poverty teaches you something very different—this is the wisdom of the immigrant.

Yuko: That's very true, and although I do not like war, and I see no solution in war, part of this began when they stopped the military draft. It's very different when you know you have to go and fight a war, or offer selfless service for the country. We have a volunteer army where 1% fight for the other 99% of the population. We've lost track of what our country stands for, we've forgotten our sense of service to this country, this democracy, and the checks and balances of government. We haven't had to fight for our country since the Vietnam War, it's been an all-volunteer army ever since then. When you talk to people who have served in the army, they have a very different mind set—they understand this selfless sacrifice very well.

Lisette: Everywhere we travel, we see the rest of the world trying to emulate the American way of life. Like when we were in Peru recently, all these little girls were trying to look like the Kardashians, which is not real life, it's a made for TV tabloid—the corrupted American dream.

Barrett: I agree with both of you, but I still believe that colonial capitalism, as an extractive system, is the real culprit behind the cultural and environmental collapse we are witnessing. The idea that you have to keep consuming, forever, whatever the product may be, creates a condition where we've replace authentic culture with a garbage heap. The only people who seem to be happy about this are the stockholders.

Yuko: I think people want to emulate America, because there used to be a real American dream. That's why people are still coming here, to make a better life, because there's still hope that they can do that here.

Lisette: Yuko, Barrett told me that you had quit practicing medicine so you could teach Zen as your full time profession. What was the moment in your life when you stopped practicing Western medicine to pursue a totally spiritual path—to study Zen? What was it that made you change the trajectory of your life so dramatically?

Yuko: I first came across meditation when I was around 18-years-old, and one of my professors at the college I went to was very settled, he was very mellow. I was really impressed by that, and I asked his son, a classmate, why his father was that way? He said that he meditated! So I tried meditating and I was amazed at the fact that it calmed me, but then I got caught up in my studies and I forgot about it. I also became more agnostic, or science-based as a premed student, but I still felt like something was missing in my life.

In going to medical school and doing my internship and residency, I saw the reality of death. I saw many people die, some in horrible ways, and I began to realize the nature of impermanence. These people just wanted to live, but they couldn't. I had also read, *The Way of Zen* by Alan Watts and I knew, with no doubt, that's what I wanted to do. Amazingly, at the same time, I read in the paper that there was a Zen master in Minneapolis, and I knew that I needed to go. I was nervous about it though, because I knew it would change my life forever.

After residency, I was offered the opportunity to join a very good medical group, and at the same time, I was doing my Zen practice. I knew then that I could not join the medical group, and I had to look deeply at my life to see what I should do.

I decided to do part time medical practice, combined with my Zen practice for 7 years, and then look at the situation to decide what to do. The more I did my Zen practice, the more I realized that, for most people, their physical suffering was coming from a deeper aspect of their being. It was a basic suffering from being dissatisfied with their life, their reality in that moment.

I was ordained as a Buddhist monk in 1982, and at the same time, I realized that being a physician gave me instant recognition. How would I know what it means in Zen to be a person of no rank, a person standing up naked in the world, with nothing to lean on such as an MD degree?

I decided in 1986 to let it all go, my medical license and my medical practice—I have never regretted that decision. I decided to just teach Buddhism and get at the basic illness that people really have, which is called ignorance, or seeing the world as divisive or dualistic, when in fact, it really isn't. This was a deeper way of looking at illness. I saw how people adhered tenaciously to their point of view, their belief systems, and this was the cause of their suffering. That is the Four Noble Truths, right there in a nutshell. That is what causes all their suffering, and that is why they get their heart attacks, high blood pressure, ulcers, anxiety, and medical or mental problems. So that is what I decided to do.

Barrett: That makes sense, because treating someone in the Emergency Room only treats their symptoms, not the source of their illness.

Lisette: How did you step into your own power Yuko? Your entire story is about leaving a professional position, which society tells you is power. Can you talk about the internal process you went through? Letting go of the money, your prestige as a doctor—what did that feel like, to make that decision and totally walk away from all of that?

Yuko: I think I was able to see a broader view of things, a broader perspective. And I was able to see life as an adventure, to see possibilities within the process itself, as opposed to a final result. That's when you realize that it's all a process, every moment, as opposed to any final thing, and this process gives you a broader perspective to be willing to go with the flow. It's amazing to just look at it and go, "Wow, that's interesting," because you would never look at it closely when you have an agenda or a path. You have to drop the construct, and then you can enjoy everything.

When you go to the supermarket, and people are putting down their groceries, you can look at other people's groceries and you can see who they really are. It is this ability that allows you to actually be connected to other people and their reality. If you are in the mindset of, "I am this person, I am this thing, I do this thing," then it's extremely painful because this sets up division, or self-centeredness. There is no self! And you have to experience what it means to stand up naked in the world, to depend on nothing, other than just your being. You know, second only to an Emergency Room, the most intense place I've ever worked is in the kitchen of a Japanese monastery. I've never seen a place more focused and precise than that.

Lisette: And that's real wisdom, when you pay attention and you experience the freedom that comes from breaking free of the construct.

Yuko. The whole practice of Zen is called dropping off body and mind, dropping off the construct of who you think you are.

Lisette: What happened after you left your medical practice to study Zen? You went to study formally in Japan, which is a radically different culture than Minnesota, where you were a doctor. How did that affect you?

Yuko: The first time I went to Japan was on a tour with our Zen teacher. I was still married at the time, and I was told I couldn't wear my wedding ring, or be in the monastery as a married woman—a married male priest was fine, but not a married woman! We toured the major monasteries, and then my teacher went back to the US, so my husband and I stayed at a temple for about two months. Then, because of other circumstances, I decided to go to another place, and the only place I could go was a women's monastery. They didn't care about doing *zazen* (silent meditation), no one spoke English, and they didn't like foreigners, so they wouldn't tell me anything. Everything was very different from my culture, so I was very homesick.

My teacher told me to stay for three months, and then when he returned he told me to stay for another three months. By then my husband had gone back home, and I thought, "No way, I can't stay here for another 3 months!" I couldn't speak the language and no one would help me, or tell me what was going on, so I had to sneak out at night to practice zazen. Things were very difficult, but my teacher was adamant that I stay, so I stayed another three months. It was a very great gift, and something changed in me—I was never home sick again, I loved Japan, and I felt very much at home there. I could finally stand up in my life.

My second time in Japan, I went to the Hosshinji Monastery and that was life-changing—my big question was answered, and that changed everything. The abbot there, Harada Sekkei Roshi, is a deeply enlightened being. His statements cut through like a sword. I had the great privilege of studying when he was there, and when I go back to Japan now, I return to Hosshinji and I feel as home there as I do in America.

Barrett: I'd love to tour Japan some day—Zen really helped me develop my musical ideas.

Yuko: That's great too, music is your way of expressing the Dharma. Remember, there are no two things in the universe! That's a really difficult thing to realize. There is no seam with your practice, so your music will teach you some things, because your music is a reflection of you. People will let you know. That's the confirmation of your life, whether you like what they have to say, or not.

Everything you do is the Dharma. It manifests in how we pick up our bowls, how we walk in the Zendo—it's all a *mudra* for constantly expressing the truth. It can manifest as a great garbageman, or a great musician, or a monk. The main thing is how you manifest *not two*, and when you resolve the Great Matter Of Life And Death, the realization is that things have always been like this. It's a constant manifestation of *not two*.

Lisette: In your many years of teaching, has there been any single thing that has been truly profound, something that is reflected your students?

Yuko: I don't see anyone as not my students, even the people at the grocery store, or the people who live in this building. I don't see only the students who come here. So you ask, is there any one thing? Hopefully I'm teaching them about *not two!* (everyone laughs)

Lisette: When you have people with whom you share this meditative path, who study and actually devote themselves to the practice, like Barrett, who continues to study. Can you see a pliancy in their mind developing as they practice, and in that process, is there a moment in which you begin to see the effects of that deepening practice?

Yuko: Yes, I feel happiness, because it's the cessation of suffering. And I feel happiness, when I experience this with others.

Barrett: Yuko, can we talk about the global environment a bit more? Because people are finally waking up to this. What do you think are the most important things we have to address with the climate crisis? Because in the last three years, Lisette and I have travelled from the Amazon to the Arctic Circle, and we've seen so much environmental damage. I've also personally seen the bleaching of the coral at the Great Barrier Reef in Australia, I've seen trees literally on fire in the Brazilian

Amazon, and I've seen entire arboreal forests in the Arctic that are literally falling over because their roots cannot hold in the melting permafrost. It is unbelievable—until you see it with your own eyes.

Lisette: Yeah, and when we were in Peru, we saw the disappearing glaciers in the Andes Mountains, and the Quechua people said they are running out of drinking water. I mean, this is radical environmental carnage that Americans and other Westerners may or may not be aware of, but the Indigenous people are. And we are part of it too—we're not separate from it. How do we get people to start talking about what is actually hapenning to our Earth?

Yuko: It's always based on awareness. Like when my assistant here started coming to help me with the sewing business in the Zendo, she was not interested in politics at all. But through our conversations, she became much more engaged with it. We have to do the same thing with the climate—you simply have to make people aware of the reality of the situation. In their daily life, they are busy taking care of their children, and all the other things that are going on in their life, so it's just a matter of awareness and dialogue. Each of us must find some way to talk with people.

I contribute to the Climate Change Project, I sign petitions about climate change, and most of the people here believe in climate change. But there are those who don't believe in climate change, so I try to explain to them what's really going on. In other words, we don't have that much time left, but with the people who don't believe this, you just have to get them to open the door a little, so they will at least look at the issue. Talk with them and become as engaged as possible, while still maintaining a centered way of life.

Here in Los Angeles we don't have much water, so I recycle the water I use for cooking noodles, to water the plants. We also have some smaller, climate-oriented power companies, so all my electricity comes from renewable green energy. As a consequence, this is starting to change the dynamics of the larger power companies. They started off by offering 25% green power, but now, because of all these little green power companies, they now offer 100% green power. It's different things like that, about how you choose to live. Do you waste things, or do you preserve things?

I have no doubt, our planet is in very dire straits, but the younger generation is tapping into this, they are really tuned in, and that's one good thing. So that's what we can do.

Lisette: This brings me to our key question: We interviewed a Cherokee healer right before we went to Peru, and a few female shamans in the Peruvian Amazon. We've also interviewed our mothers, and we went up to Alaska to interview an Indigenous professor, and some artists and performers in New York and New Mexico. One of the patterns we keep hearing in these women's stories, is that the structures they grew up in were male-dominated systems of power. So my question for you is, how do we reach a balance between the masculine and the feminine roles in things like business, economics, education, politics?

Yuko: In Zen, it is the balance of wisdom, the masculine aspect, embodied as the Buddha Manjushri, combined with the feminine aspect, which is compassion, embodied as the Buddha Avalokiteshvara. The balance between the two, is the ability of a person to become Manjushri, which is the ability to be assertive and unyielding, fearless, and not intimidated or shaken in any way. Compassion, or the part that sees all beings as their children is Avalokiteshvara, which is an allowing process. The masculine is assertive, and the feminine side is more allowing, more inclusive, less egoistic. Manjushri is very selfless and not swayed or deluded by opinions, and the compassionate Avalokiteshvara enjoys this, which allows a being to flower. It just wants the situation to work, to function—it wants the whole process to work.

Also, the translation of Avalokiteshvara is that he/she is the regarder of the cries of the world, so you have to be willing to hear that. A lot of people don't want to hear that, because there's something incredibly painful about it. But you must be willing to hear that incredible sound, which is allowing the other being, or situation, to be there, totally, as opposed to creating a framework where you expect everything to happen according to your map, or conceptual framework. It's like being a mother—the mother listens to what her child needs.

I tutor children a lot, and the kids will always tell you where they're at. You can tell when the kids are done studying, when they can't absorb anymore. They will communicate what they need, and what they are capable of. The feminine allows that process to happen, so a human being is the merging of those two things, wisdom and compassion, and the realizing of *not two* allows you to function as both. You see things clearly, and you allow it to be there.

Buddhism is the merging of these two elements, but you have to drop your conceptual framework to allow this to happen. When we cross a bridge, we think of it as a bridge—I have to cross it. But in reality, the bridge is asking you to cross it. The bridge is actually saying to you, "Please cross me—that makes me a bridge!" The world is always speaking to us, but we don't usually hear it unless it fits our agenda or conceptual framework.

Barrett: That's exactly what I learned from the Gwich'in people up in the Arctic National Wildlife Refuge. I went up into the mountains with one of their caribou hunters and he said to me, "I don't hunt the caribou—they come to me, and they present themselves, and these are the ones that want to give their life to the people. I only shoot the caribou who offer themselves as food—and only them."

Yuko: Yes, that's very Zen. Things are doing that all the time, we just don't see it because we are locked in our mental constructs, but it's happening all over the place. That's what you come to realize, the whole world operates that way but we have our blinders on, and when something opens up we don't see it, but if you are open to it, it's totally visible. It's beautiful how in touch Native people are with these things, but everything is like that, all the time.

Lisette: I have heard shamans say that the universe is always communicating with us, giving us these signs, showing us the opportunities to follow a magical path—to cross that bridge! And I have heard Buddhist teachers talk about energetic waves, whereby maculine or feminine energies can become more dominant for a time, and during such times of imbalance, a particular ignorance will reign.

Yuko: When you look at the masculine aspect in Asian society, it's very different. They're not as rational in their way of approaching things. The West is based more on Aristotle and the rational point of view, whereas the Asian view is much more holistic and it embraces non-rational thinking. It's not interested in a linear way of looking at things, it looks at things holistically. English words are very straightforward and rational, but in Japanese, a single word has behind it the thing you are looking at, and maybe the time of day, so it has this dimensionality. They see the wholeness of things, whereas Western society categorizes and separates things.

The Eastern mind is able to incorporate the feminine, allowing an inclusive aspect into themselves, but the Western mind does not translate in the same way. We can see this with how Western medicine views the body—they can't see the holistic aspect of the body, they just see the anatomy of the heart, but not the emotional and spiritual aspects of the heart. It took them years to accept the reality of acupuncture, or the existence of the chakras, which are of course, very real things.

Lisette: It seems like we are finally starting to merge the Eastern and Western minds. The Western world's gift is our technology and our ability to organize people, and the greatest gift of the Eastern world is meditation, and Buddhism in general. It's the ability to look inwardly, and truly learn how the mind functions in the world. It'd be amazing to unify those two things for all beings.

Yuko: Wait till you see what happens with quantum physics! The quantum entanglement theory is totally Buddhism, right there. I'm just starting to understand Einstein's theory of relativity, and I'm amazed that he believed in the independent existence of a thing. He believed in locality and boundary, but he couldn't see that there is no boundary or source. Quantum physics bothered him a lot, but he knew it was a reality.

When they start looking at time in order to understand quantum physics, they are going to have to look into the realm of the metaphysical, because the scientific method, that is, the conceptual framework, cannot understand what the universe really is. It will not work the way they think it should, because the universe functions in non-conceptual reality, and the universe doesn't see differences as separate. We do, and that's our biggest problem with perception, in that we perceive difference as separate.

A Buddha is someone who doesn't perceive difference as separate. A Buddha sees things, but does not perceive them. Perceiving means, "I can see something over there," and that's wrong. That's creating two things, and there are no two things! That's what our mind does. We came down out of the trees as monkeys, and our mind was a protective mechanism that said, "This thing is over here, and that thing is over there," but in reality there is no *over there.*

Anyway, they're going to prove that quantum physics works at the galactic level too. They are going to see that there is no source, no two things operating everywhere, as we can see with quantum entanglement. The particles communicate instantly over vast distances because they are not separate from each other, and not because they appear to exceed the speed of light. That's what our conceptual framework does—it sees differences and then, superfast, it creates the idea that a thing is over there—it creates the illusion of separateness. Quantum physics is Buddhism to a T!"

Barrett: The Large Hadron Collider in Europe has been testing those two theories, looking for unity between them, and finding out about a lot of other things in the process. That is exactly where the merging of the scientific method, and the Buddha mind of seeing will take place, although I doubt they are thinking about Zen while they are doing their experiments!

Yuko: But you need the Buddha mind to see it. They are trying to find the Unified Field Theory, but they don't realize that they already have it, with the two different actions of physics: the subatomic, or quantum field, and the larger object actions at the atomic level. They see them as separate—but they aren't.

Look at Stephen Hawking, who was just incredible, and he postulated that there was a multiverse. Do you know what his last paper was about before he died? He decided that there were too many universes and there should be a limit on universes! How can you have a limit on universes—who's limit? This is what our minds do, especially when it's working with numbers and formulas—we want to create a construct.

That's how strongly we want our own, personal framework to be imposed on something. Quantum physics is going to blow people's minds, and yet it's so Zen it's unbelievable—that a particular thing can be generated out of nothingness, out of a vacuum, and that there is no beginning or end to the universe.

This is going to be part of the New Awakening, it's going to be in physics, but not just physics, it's also in metaphysics.

It's going to be the merging of the two.

THE ARTISTS

Alma Martinez

Singer, Dancer & Mother

"My mother would really make me notice the world of women, and in Latin America they have a kind of magic, in that they make society function in every kind of intimate way, as well as in the bigger picture."

-Lila Downs

Lisette: I wake up some mornings and I wonder if I've done enough with my life. It's a gift, life, and I'm not certain that I've relished each moment enough. Have I done enough for the progress of women, Latinas, humans, all beings, the Earth itself? If I continue that line of questioning, surely I'll come up short. I'm not famous, and I'm not especially good at any one thing, but I have lived life my own way, untraditionally and even radically. I have been blessed to have amazing people around me, and I've been blessed to love—really love. I have my mother to thank for creating that potential.

My mother was told that she was expecting twins, but it was just me when I came out into the world. In a family where names are all shared and recycled, I was given my name from the TV Guide, and I've often wondered if some part of my mother unconsciously wanted a different life for me.

My earliest memory of my mother is of her singing an extremely upbeat lullaby that she had written just for me, "Esta niña tan bonita, no me deja descansar. Ya se pone a reír. Ya se pone a llorar...."

My mother was beautiful and talented, and if she had had a different life, the artist in her would have been more nurtured. But the artist's life was not a proper thing for a decent, young, Mexican woman to strive for back then. Her mother had been one of 14 girls, and during the time of Pancho Villa, they all had their particular hiding places. Once Pancho Villa and his men took their leave, my great grandmother would account for each daughter, while praying that their honor was still intact.

There were very clear lines of impropriety back then, and my mother was still held to those standards. When she immigrated to the United States upon marrying my father, she was as naive as a modern day 5-year-old in the realm of the birds and the bees. She did her best to master the English language, and to try and understand American culture. By the time my sister and I were born, my mother had fully assimilated to the point that for us kids, speaking English properly was a must and Spanglish was a natural thing. Culturally, however, we were still very Mexican. The food we ate, the music we listened to, the way we danced, the focus on family, and a belief in hard work were characteristics that were deeply valued and ingrained in each of us, genetically perhaps, straight from our motherland.

When my father left the family, my mother fell to pieces—it was terrible. When the shock finally wore off, she began to look for a job and find ways to improve herself. She ended up doing very well for herself and finally, later in life, she was able to dedicate herself to her greatest love—singing and dancing.

My mother is known for her generosity and her passion, which is exemplified best in her soulful *grito*. The Mexican people can be very passionate and the grito is a show of that emotion, especially when traditional music is being played. A Mexican will feel sorrow or joy to the depths of their being, which makes the grito as political as it is emotional. It has been used to hail the beginnings of wars, the ends of them, and individual freedom as well. Not just anyone can do it, but my mother—she's got one of the best.

Our conversation took place in the same modest El Paso home where I grew up, near the Texas-Mexico border, where the lights of Juarez, Mexico are clearly visible in the distance beyond the fence line.

Lisette: Mama, what was it like growing up in Mexico before you came to the United States? You were very young when you immigrated here, so what did that feel like?

Alma: Well, I had never thought about coming to the US—never. I had a good job working as a secretary at the chamber of commerce in Juarez. My responsibilities included taking dictation, typing out letters, and I had to know all the people who worked there. It didn't pay very much, and my mom used to say to me, "I sent you to school and all you make is 34 pesos a week?" It was my father, who was working as a driver for the city engineers, who got me my next job. The chamber of commerce changed their employees a lot, and my father said it was because people would just sit there and not do anything. He said, "The minute they tell you to quit, you just quit!" Then he got me a job at the engineering office. It was really great—they paid 2-3 times more than what I was getting at the chamber of commerce.

Lisette: How long were you at that job?

Alma: Only about a year or so. That's where I met a lot of my boyfriends! (everyone laughs)

Lisette: Que bonitos recuerdos! Did you like anyone in particular?

Alma: There was one boy named Manuel that I really liked, but he was quite a bit older than me. When I met your dad and we got married, Manuel came to the wedding and he made a little bit of a scene!

Lisette: Mom, you never told me about this—this is scandalous!

Barrett: Ha ha! The jealous ex-boyfriend shows up! How many people came to your wedding Alma, I bet it was huge?

Alma: A lot of people—a lot! I was still very young, and I wasn't planning on getting married, but when I met Lisette's father, I recall him saying to me, "Listen, you're old enough now." He was very handsome and kind, and he really swept me off my feet. But to be honest, back in those days, if you met a young man that could take care of you and who seemed to be from a good family, then that was enough.

His mother came to the wedding from the US, as well as his sister Lupe and her husband. They drove all the way from Dallas to Juarez for the wedding.

Lisette: How long had you and dad dated by that point?

Alma: Not long, maybe 6 months.

Barrett: Well, I'm glad you got married because we got Lisette out of the deal!

Alma: My parents were very happy that I was getting married, but my mother said to me, "OK, if you're going to get married, I don't want to hear any complaints at all—never! Unless he leaves you for another woman or he hits you, then I want to know." Fortunately, for many years our marriage was a good one.

Lisette: So dad married you and brought you to the US. Where did you move to, and how did you live?

Alma: He was in the United States Air Force, so we rented a little apartment in Dallas. At first, we didn't have anything, so my mom gave us a pan with a lid, and we used the lid as a plate! It was a very simple yet exciting time—it was fun actually.

Lisette: At that time you didn't speak any English, so how did you find work, what did you do?

Alma: Your dad didn't want me to work at all, and I never really worked until the end of our marriage. I couldn't speak English at first, and when we'd go to the movies, his brother Julio would laugh at me and say, "You just laugh when everybody else laughs!" It used to upset me a lot, but it was true. I had to learn English—and fast.
Your dad and Julio were brought up as twins, even though they were actually uncle and nephew, because they were so close in age. They say your dad's mother fed them both at the same time, they always shared everything, and that's why it was so hard for your father when Julio died. He was just too young.

Lisette: What did you think about the differences in culture between the US and Mexico back then? Was it hard to make the change from Mexican to American culture?

Alma: No, it was easy. My mother-in-law liked me, and she taught me how to do everything. Her daughters were born in the US, and since I knew Spanish so well, we would trade lessons back and forth. I would teach them Spanish, and they would teach me English. Nowadays, I'm speaking more Spanish again, so I think I am forgetting my English, but in those days, they were proud to introduce me and say, "She is from Mexico, but she can speak English very well!" It was a good life.

Lisette: And you had your first child after being married for two years. What was it like being a new mom?

Alma: We were renting a place next door to your father's mom. It only had two extra rooms—a kitchen and a bathroom. Junior was a perfect baby and little boy. He was strong, handsome, and good at everything he did.

I was always happy with whatever your father could give us, and then for the longest time, I didn't have any more children until your sister Carmelita came along 15 years later, and then you came after that. It was very painful for me during those 15 years between you kids, because I wasn't able to bring another baby to full term. I kept losing them, it was agony. Your father and I both came from large families, and although that is what we wanted, it just wasn't in the cards for us.

Lisette: What was it like during those early years in Texas? Because by the time all three of us kids were born, dad was already a full time school teacher, and you were now raising three kids. Well two kids actually, because Junior was already 18-years-old by the time I was born.

Alma: I would help you all with your homework, in fact, I was really good at typing, so I typed out all of Junior's papers. I was also very good at math, and I was pretty good at spelling. I knew how to write English well, how to conjugate the verbs, perhaps because English was my second language.

Barrett: My mom is always correcting my spelling, even though I'm a pretty good speller too! Alma, do you remember the first time you felt discriminated against, for being Mexican, or a woman, or both?

Alma: Yes, it was a different era, a time when there were signs on drinking fountains that read, "No dogs, no Mexicans." One time after my husband had become a schoolteacher, he had to go to Dallas for some meetings. He asked me to join him, and I had Junior with me, although he was still a little boy at the time. We all went to Dallas together and I remember that I needed to go to the store to get something, and there were these stairs going up to the store. There were a lot of white women sitting on the stairs, so I said, "Excuse me", but they ignored me and they refused to move. I thought, maybe they didn't hear me, so I said it again, "Excuse me, please!" but they refused to let me pass. I finally just jumped over one of them and I went on my way. I told your dad about it, and I felt kind of strange, because I had never been discriminated against before, and I didn't really understand why someone would even do that. My husband just told me, "Never ask those bitches for anything!"

Barrett: That is exactly right, Mamacita!

Lisette: So this happened after dad left the Air Force and he graduated from college on the GI Bill, and then he became a history teacher, right?

Alma: Yes, you see he originally wanted to work on the family farm, but his family said, "Look, you can't make any money doing this, because your brothers will all want their shares from you."

Lisette: That explains a lot! I even remember the time when the animals from the farm were brought to our house in El Paso. We kept them in the back yard, and we learned how to milk the cows and you made cheese and chorizo. When his family decided against him taking over the family farm, what happened next?

Alma: He was naturally very smart, so they talked him into going to college on the GI Bill after he got out of the Air Force. He got a teaching job in El Paso, and that's when we bought this land for $1,000 and we began building our house.

During the summer vacation from school he was still getting paid, so we bought the land with those wages and he started building the house that summer. He had all his friends come over to help pour the foundation, do the framing, and that's the same house I still live in today. That's where Carmelita and Lisette were born.

Lisette: That's the only house we ever knew. What was it like, finally having your own house?

Alma: Oh I loved it, but of course there was a lot of work that still had to be done on the inside. All the walls were painted the same color, and the floors had the same kind of tile, because it was cheaper to finish the house that way.

Lisette: And you still loved music and dancing—you were known to be a great singer in Juarez. Did you keep singing and dancing when you moved to Texas?

Alma: I did, and my cousin Sylvia used to say to me, "How did you know you could sing?" I remember back to when I was about 4-years-old and my Tia (aunt) would ask me to sing outside her window on summer nights. She would sit on the other side of the window with her boyfriend, and they would have a romantic date with me singing in the background. About the same time, I won my first contest for singing on the radio in Juarez, and I was so proud because I won a gallon of *leche* (milk)!

Then when I was about 11 or 12-years-old, there was a young lady who lived a couple houses down from my mother, and she had parties all the time. She would call my mother and ask if I could come sing at her party, so I would put on a nice dress, my best shoes, and I'd go sing songs for everyone at the party. Afterwards, I would just walk home and go straight to bed.

Barrett: That is awesome! You were singing at parties right out of the gate—a natural born entertainer!

Lisette: And when you married dad, did you keep on singing?

Alma: Yes, I used to sing a lot, for everybody. I was always singing, I guess because I was a happy person.

Lisette: So 15 years after your first child was born came Carmelita, the miracle baby. I came last, the final storm. I was born on Easter Sunday, I love that fact.

Barrett: Alma, what was the feeling you had about Lisette when she was a baby?

Alma: Lisette was always trying to figure things out! If it was a radio, she wanted to know who was singing inside the radio—why was the radio singing, how did it work? She would take the radio apart and look inside of it, but she wasn't always able to put it back together!
We used to have a big living room with about ten chairs around the big dining room table, and whenever I couldn't find Lisette, I would run around the house looking for her. I knew she had done something naughty, but I could never find her because she would be lying across the seats of chairs, hiding under the table! (everyone laughs)

Lisette: It was amazing to have a home and a safe place to play and run around, and the most important thing to remember is that you were able to buy that land, build your own home, and own everything without a mortgage. It wasn't that long ago really, it was the 1970s, and people didn't have any real debt, or at least very little. Now everything: mortgages, student loans, cars loans, credit cards, the entire financial system is designed to deliberately put people into debt. We're watching that system destroy our country, right now.

Alma: Back then, if you wanted to buy something, you had to save up for it. If I had to buy shoes for the children, maybe they cost ten dollars a pair, and they only got them right before school started, or maybe at Christmas. I would make the same dresses for both of you girls and people would say, "Que bonitas!" I was so proud of my sewing.

Barrett: Alma, your name literally means *soul* in Spanish, which is perfect for a singer and dancer like you. What is it about Mexican folkloric music that makes it so unique in the world? I remember studying it a little bit in school—it's just so beautiful. We don't have anything like that in the United States, so we invented blues, jazz, rock & roll, and everything else. But Mexican folkloric music really stands out as a beautiful, unique form of world music. What inspired you to sing and dance it?

Alma: It was the music—I just loved the music! And the dresses are so beautiful and colorful, it just makes you want to dance. You know, there were only two things that I really wanted to do in life: One, I wanted to sing and do folkloric dancing, and two, I wanted to work in real estate. I did both! I was part of a folkloric dance troupe that performed all around Texas, and I also got my real estate license. I would take photos of our performances and show the people at the real estate office, and I would invite our customers to our dance performances. It was the perfect melding of my two dreams.

The dancing wasn't about showing off either, it all has deep cultural meaning, but I just loved the music. I could feel the music coming up through my feet and I just had to dance—I had to dance! I would yell out the grito when the music began, and this would inspire all the other dancers.

Lisette: How many years did you dance total?

Alma: I danced for about 13 years, maybe a little more than that. I was always the oldest person in the troupe, and I was very proud of that fact.

Lisette: And what do you think is the most important thing you can pass on to young people coming into the world today? Like, what is your message to the next generation of young people and artists?

Alma: Just be a good person, and work really hard—and do the right things. Especially if you come to the United States, you have to work really hard. I had a good husband and he didn't want me to work, but I worked a couple of times over the years when we needed to buy something, like a washer and dryer or a piece of furniture, and then I would work for a few months until we could buy it with cash.

Life was very simple back then. We all had breakfast together every morning, then their father would go off to work, and the kids would walk to school. We were all together at the end of the day, which is how I thought it would always be. Now, with more than 80 years under my belt, I know one thing for sure—nothing ever plays out exactly the way you think it will.

There will be tragedy, deep pain, growth, and above all, intense love.

Deana Martin

Musician, Homesteader, & Mother

"The real things haven't changed. It is still best to be honest and truthful, to make the most of what we have, to be happy with simple pleasures, and have courage when things go wrong."

–Laura Ingalls Wilder

Barrett: When I think about my mother, it is usually surrounded by the memory of the land where I grew up. It was a forested 5½ acres of first growth forest, several miles south of the Washington State capitol of Olympia. I was still a little kid at the time, but I remember my parents clearing some of the land to build a ranch-style house with enough space on either side for a couple of large gardens, and even a bit of pastureland for our horses and other animals. There remained a forest of diverse trees around the perimeter of the land, primarily of cedar, Douglas fir, pine, hemlock, maple, alder, and even a grove of oak trees that remained unbowed in the center of the pasture. There was also a wetlands nearby, and some of the land would flood in the winter, where a large drainage system would channel the runoff. In the summers, thousands of frogs and numerous birds would croak and chirp late into the night.

My mother, in her high school and college years, had been a violinist, and she later worked for her father's business, which was a flying school at the Olympia airport. After the business was sold in the 1970s, she became more of a stay at home mom, keeping me and my siblings occupied with a variety of artistic endeavors that ranged from painting, to sculpting, to writing our own stories, and always some kind of musical play.

My mom had gone to a liberal arts college, although she never finished her degree because of her marriage to my father, and the ensuing responsibilities of raising a young family. Still, my general memory of that time was of artistic creativity in the home—and a long list of perpetual chores to be done around the homestead in which we thrived.

Growing up in the rural 1970s and 80s on the far outskirts of what was already a small, sleepy town, my life could not have been more, well, sleepy. I enjoyed walking around in the forest, and the easy ability to swim in the local lakes and ponds, perhaps catching a fish, target practice with my bow & arrow, and all the various things that kids did before the age of the Internet. As I got older, I couldn't wait to move to the big city of Seattle and beyond, but I still appreciated a life growing up in the woods of the Pacific Northwest. In many ways, it was an idyllic way to live, close to the land, close to the food we grew, and close to the animals that served as pets—and also sometimes as food.

I learned a few survival skills along the way too, like how to navigate the forest, make a camp, fall a dead tree for firewood, and how to build a fire—things most northwesterners learned naturally. And like most of us, my first teachers were my mother and grandmother. They were the ones closest to me, and in my case, I was fortunate to have both of them as my earliest teachers. This was largely because my parents and grandparents also worked together in the family's flying business.

As a child, I was shuttled back and forth between them all, and I became as close with my grandparents as I was to my own parents. Although my grandmother died young, she was a huge source of inspiration to us all, because she loved music, she sang and played piano, and she wrote poetry on a regular basis.

Fortunately my mom was very much the same way, so Lisette and I used the opportunity of this book to ask her about her early artistic aspirations, before she began raising three kids in the relative wilderness, a decision which changed the course of her life.

We sat down at her home in the southernmost waters of the Salish Sea in Washington State, on a piece of land that has been in my family for generations. I started with a joke about how, after being a professional musician my entire life, it is a comical truth that my first musical tours with the Tumwater High School Thunderbird Jazz Ensemble included my mother as one of the chaperones. If you knew some of the rougher bands I went on to play with, this is actually quite funny.

Lisette: Deana, when we talked with my mother, Alma, she talked about how people, and even immigrants, didn't have any debt back then. In fact, several of the other women we have interviewed have brought up how different the economy is today, and how there used to be much more cash circulating between people before the creation of household debt in the 1980s. What do you remember about money back in the 1960s and 70s, because young people need to know this?

Deana: Right, well back in those days, no one had any real debt or even credit cards, because people lived within their means, with the cash they had on hand. If you wanted to buy something on a payment plan, you just did layaway at the local department store. Or you saved— nobody saves anymore, or they don't make enough to save anything after all the bills are paid.

Lisette: The economics of the world were certainly much simpler back then. Can you share how you met your husband, Brian?

Deana: I met Brian in high school, here in Olympia. We both went to Olympia High School. I saw him playing in the school orchestra and I fell in love at first sight. I was the principle violinist in the city orchestra, and I was also in the Latin club. Who studies Latin anymore—I did!

After I graduated, I spent one year at the University of Puget Sound, but then we decided to get married before we finished college. I moved to Seattle where Brian was finishing a bachelor's degree in political science at the University of Washington. We lived in a 30 foot Airstream trailer near the campus, and since I had dropped out of college, I got a job working for Boeing Aircraft, while Brian worked as a waiter at a Swedish restaurant.

Once he graduated, we spent all of our money on a three-month trip around Europe. This was in 1964, so it was the coolest time to go to Europe, and we survived on a tourist budget of just $5.00 a day—you could actually do that back then!

The Vietnam War had also started, and in the beginning, alot of us thought it was a legitimate thing for the United States to get involved in the war. Brian was really inspired by JFK and his call to serve the country in any way that you could, so after we got back from Europe, he volunteered because he wanted to serve. Unfortunately he was rejected because of a hearing problem, but after that initial setback, he got a job working for Washington State. Then we bought what I think was the nicest home we ever owned, which was ironically our first home. It was on a small lake called Pattison Lake, and it cost all of $24,000 back in 1964. Looking back, I don't know why we sold it, but we did, and we moved into yet another house, which was a stylish A-Frame built on a golf course near another lake known as Scott Lake.

Barrett: I remember the Scott Lake house because that's where we lived when the Apollo moon landings were happening. I remember watching them on a black and white TV in the upstairs loft, I must have only been 5 or 6-years-old.

Deana: Well, we didn't stay there for very long either, because we were the youngest people in the neighborhood, and we were never really accepted or welcomed by the older, golf course types. So we made the move out to the woods, because we wanted to live with the animals and the birds—with the critters!

Lisette: That must have been a big change for you as a young couple. Was it all you had wished for, what was it like?

Deana: Part of the decision was because my side of the family had been farmers and miners. My mother remembered the stories of how both sides of her family had suffered terribly during the Dust Bowl of the 1930s, when their farms were destroyed by the loss of the topsoil. She remembers seeing logbooks of the items that her family had to sell at the auctions, as they gave up their farms in Kansas and Nebraska. I was born in Colorado, and then the family came west to California and eventually up to the Pacific Northwest, so part of me wanted to remember what it was like to live close to the land, rather than in a city.

Brian and I had saved up enough cash to buy a 5½ acre parcel, which we purchased from two brothers, the Pedersen Brothers, who were actual cowboys from Missouri. They had bought a few hundred acres of land in the forest, way back when it was still cheap. We paid $5,000 for our parcel and we immediately set out to clear the land for the house site. The land had been logged probably a hundred years earlier by the first settlers at the end of the Oregon Trail, which ends in Olympia, by the way. Some of the largest, older trees still had chain scars gouged into their upper reaches, which meant they had been used as spars by loggers in the early 1900s. The spars were anchor points, by which they dragged the fallen trees out of the forest, because they would have been using horse teams back then. But there were still some huge trees left standing, so we consciously left all of the large cedar and Douglas fir trees untouched, and we only cleared the small alders and other scraggly trees.

Barrett: I remember those huge trees—they were magnificent. I guess some of those pioneers must have felt it was important to leave a few of them standing, maybe out of respect for their ancientness. You'd never find that kind of intellingence in a modern logging corporation today—they'd just clear-cut everything. OK, so what was the next phase of the house building?

Deana: Well, we set about burning enormous piles of brush around the area where the house was going to be built. With the cleared pastureland, it added up to about one full acre that we cleared, so the vast majority of the forest was left intact, with walking trails that we created for long walks and exploration.

Lisette: There was a social trend back then for people to move back to the land and get off the grid, and we are seeing this again today. I grew up in a city, but my father always had farm animals, and we didn't always understand that they weren't just pets. We had goats, rabbits, pigs, and cows. I find those circular trends so interesting—back and forth between city and nature.

Deana: Our parents also loved that we were doing this. I remember the smell of the land, and specifically the old nurse logs from the giant trees, which had fallen decades earlier and helped to create a landscape that was full of new trees, trillium lilies, and even huckleberry and salmonberry, which are edible berries. The entire forest was filled with these enormous sword ferns, which are those giant prehistoric looking things that could grow a few feet in height, covering the entire forest floor. It was totally like an ancient landscape, like the movie *Jurassic Park*.

We also had yipping coyotes out there, friendly but wily raccoons, and there was a mother black bear that at one point had a couple of cubs. We saw their tracks on the old dirt logging road that ran parallel to the property. There was also at least one porcupine, as our dog unfortunately found out.

Barrett: Yep, I remember pulling the porcupine quills from her nose, and when you took us kids to see the bear tracks—we were scared but fascinated.

Deana: I also subscribed to Mother Earth Magazine, which had articles about how to cut firewood, raise goats, and other such things that a back-to-the-land family would need to know. That's where I got the idea for planting two gardens on either side of the house—one for the ground vegetables, and the other for berries and taller, stalk-growing vegetables. We had raspberries which, when they finally matured, gave us huge amounts of berries every day—it seemed to be an endless supply. There was also a giant wall of wild blackberries farther down the old logging road, where all the neighborhood kids would go pick bucket loads of blackberries for their mothers to bake into pies.

We also raised several animals, such as the aforementioned goats, which we used to clear more brush—they would eat everything in sight, down to the bare dirt, wherever they were staked out. Our first pig, Lucy, was highly intelligent, and she became this enormous, friendly hog that your sister Amy would ride around in the yard, whenever she wasn't riding her horse. And Brandon raised a couple of sheep, which we slaughtered when they were full-grown, much to his life-long resentment.

We also had chickens that we got at a local feed store, which we raised for slaughter, and that was a traumatizing and messy affair for you kids. But I suppose the other side of it, is that it's good to know where your food is coming from!

Barrett: Oh yes, I remember that gruesome affair....

Deana: And of course we had the horses and various dogs and cats, so within a short amount of time, our homestead was pretty functional with gardens, a small orchard, and a bit of an animal farm. We got our butter from a small dairy up the road, and the Pederson Brothers taught us how to be beekeepers, so we made our own honey.

Lisette: Olympia has a rather famous farmer's market too—I heard you had something to do with that?

Deana: I was one of the first two people to be invited to the Olympia Farmers Market, which was held in the parking lot of the local Shakey's Pizza Parlor. My friend Barb and I would load the Vista Cruiser station wagon and sell our vegetables and honeycomb for a few dollars, right out of the tailgate of the wagon.

Barrett: I also remember that we went to a Methodist church, but only for a few years. It was Christianty-light and the people were very cool. The best part was the potluck buffet at the end of Sunday service, when everyone stood around eating and talking. I remember they were all great people, and fortunately, Olympia has always been a liberal town. I guess liberal Christianity was a thing back then?

Deana: The best church around us was that Methodist church, and the best part of it was that the pastor's wife was a true feminist, without outwardly espousing it. She just led all of us women by example, and that was just great—we really loved her!

My mother was a natural feminist too. She had two other sisters, she was the middle of the three, and they were all gorgeous, musically talented, and indepedent. Back then, when the boys would come around to court them, instead of asking them to bring flowers or candy, they would insist that they bring sheet music instead. They had a piano, and all three sisters could play and sing.

You know, my mother was really beautiful, but she had been in a car wreck as a young girl, which put a permanent scar across her chin. Some girls at her high school gave her the cruel nickname of *Scarface*, nevertheless, she made the cheerleading team four years in a row and was offered a full scholarship for her academic abilities. This was in the early 1940s, when it was uncommon for working class women to attend college, much less on a scholarship.

She was married at 17 and a mother by 19, so she and I had more of a sisterly relationship, being relatively close in age. She ran the family business, Vagabond Aviation, which was one of the first flight schools in Olympia that your grandfather started in 1967. She had incredibly progressive views for a woman of that post-war era, and people just loved her for that. She was so generous and kind to everyone, but she was also tough when it came to work—no slouching around her!

Lisette: So Deana, you saw your own creativity manifest as a homesteader rather than as a musician. You're out there in the forest, with gardens that grew enough food to feed your entire family, with enough left over to sell at the Farmers Market. What else did you do to stay creative?

Deana: Well, it was the 1970s, so we did a lot of arts and crafts with the kids, and even with the other neighborhood kids. Every magazine had all these craft ideas: we painted, we sculpted, we did knitting and macramé, and we made all kinds of things for the house—picnic tables, chairs, we built decks, bird houses, things for the garden. My father and I built a barn for the horses, and Barrett had his drums set up in the hayloft.

Barrett: Yep, I remember there was always some kind of project going on, in various stages of completion. Plus we had that gigantic, antique player-piano and all those old musical instruments, so there was always live music happening. It was a fun time, and I think the spirit of creativity was really alive in our house, which is why all the neighborhood parties were held there!

Deana: We always had a few of the neighborhood kids at the house too, who we would feed at lunch and dinner time. That's just how it was back then—the families around us didn't have much money either, and some of those kids were hungry more often than not. I always felt that I may not be able to save anyone, but I can always cook a good meal and make a person feel better right then. We just fed whoever was hanging around the house at dinnertime, with whatever food we had.

Lisette: Let's talk about food for a little bit—I am Mexican after all! Because we are now entering a period of time where food might become scarcer with climate change, and we can't even trust the quality of the food that comes from big corporations. What do you think about that?

Deana: Well, we must be able to trust our food supply again, which we can't anymore with all the pesticides and preservatives the corporations use. So people really need to learn to grow a bit of their own food, as much as they can. And we really have to get off the fossil fuel addiction. I mean, I grew up with cars and airplanes in the 1960s, but having lived through the oil crisis of the 1970s, and now with global warming and the climate crisis, it is clearly not a sustainable or healthy form of energy, and that has to change. We probably need to move to electric vehicles and electricity as a sustainable energy supply—not coal or oil, which is a 19th century form of energy.

Lisette: Deana, you're way more radical than I thought!

Deana: Well, I just really think that every person should have a basic understanding of agriculture and aquaculture, even if you work in an office. At a foundational level, everyone should know this stuff, so that you can always grow some food and get clean water for your family. You just can't rely on the system anymore—the systems are breaking down.

And you know, I actually did work in an office at one point. Back in 1980, when we sold Vagabond Aviation and you kids were in the upper grades of school, I decided that I wanted to grow myself a little more. I was always interested in medicine, so I enrolled in the Medical Assistant course at South Puget Sound College. I discovered that I really loved to learn, and I totally aced all of my tests! After graduation, I managed the front office for a British general surgeon for almost a decade, until we moved to Australia in 1991—that's when your dad got transferred down there.

Australia provided yet another huge opportunity for growth, because after half a century of life in little Olympia, we had this chance to go and live on an entirely different continent. The kids were all on their own by that point, so I had to pack up the family homestead and sell it, sell our vehicles, and sell off the remaining animals. It was sad, but it was also exciting, because getting outside of your comfort zone is where real growth happens.

Just getting my Australian driver's license and learning how to drive on the left side of the road, in a city of over 4 million people—that was a huge thing for me. I could finally drive in the city, and I could pop over the Sydney Harbor Bridge with ease.

It ended up being a six-year assignment for us, when Brian was promoted to the Chief Operating Officer of an explosives company that worked with all the Australian and New Zealand mining companies. When he wasn't working, we traveled extensively, visiting all of the incredible national parks in both of those countries. A couple of times we even traveled back to Europe—it was a lot different from when we were there in 1964! My world became truly global, and I learned to appreciate that the moon I saw in the Southern Hemisphere, was also seen by my family in Washington State.

I also became part of a women's traveling group—we called ourselves *The Intrepids*. We would travel together and really expore the far flung corners of Australia and New Zealand, doing eco-camping and seeing all the exotic landscapes and animals.

I really tried to learn about the Indigenous people in those places, about their history, and the horrible things they had endured during colonization and beyond. You know, my dad was part Cherokee Indian and I always felt a little of that in me, so I really tried to learn as much as I could about the Aboriginal and Maori peoples.

Anyway, you can imagine how much that affected me, a small town girl from Olympia, suddenly living in cosmopolitan Sydney, and all the things I was exposed to. It was so vastly different from Washington State, and I'd like to think that it turned me into a better woman.

Barrett: Yeah, I remember visiting you and dad in Australia, and also touring with my bands down there. I thought, wow, this is a completely different way of life than growing up in the sticks of Washington. But it also shows how a person's life can change so quickly and dramatically, if you're open to it.

Deana: I also think we need to stop thinking that we are alone in the universe, and we need to start thinking about the other forms of life that most certainly exist out there in the cosmos. The Indigenous people talked about this all the time, it's in all their ancient myths and stories.

Barrett: Mom, now you're talking about aliens!

Deana: They're out there…. (everyone laughs)

Lisette: We agree! If the factors necessary for life have come together here on Earth, chances are that it has happened somewhere else too. Statistically, it's a no-brainer that there is alien life out there. OK Deana, what about your grandkids, of which you have five now. What do you have to say to the younger generations?

Deana: Well, I'm a little worried that they won't have the same opportunities that my generation had. Economically and environmentally, things are a lot worse for them than they were for us. That bothers me a lot, as well as the rising oceans and lack of clean water from global warming and industrial pollution. We're sitting here on the banks of Puget Sound, but this home will eventually be underwater, maybe not so far in the distant future. It really bothers me that we are not addressing climate change right now, while we still have time.

Lisette: So what are the highest qualities and attitudes that you think young people need to embrace now, in order to cope with this uncertain future?

Deana: We have to learn how to celebrate the differences between people, and we also have to learn how to communicate better. And I really believe that means eliminating all the vulgarity in the way people speak to each other these days. It just doesn't go anywhere to insult people and make fun of them—you just end up sounding like a very ignorant person!
A person needs to develop an inquisitive and questioning mind, and you have to be mindful of how you interact with other people, especially with the kind of work you do in the world. So don't do any kind of work that destroys the Earth—do things that help it grow and become beautiful again.
This also means you cannot allow sloth to enter into your life, which means maintaining self-control. You cannot let yourself be pulled into anything that's addictive or destructive. Americans have become so addicted to everything—alcohol, drugs, junkfood, shopping, vanity— we don't even know how to feed or educate ourselves anymore!

Lisette: What about the creative things, like art and the music you loved to play?

Deana: Of course, I think making art and playing music is a highly important thing for every person to do, even if it's just a hobby. Learn how to paint, or sculpt, or play a musical instrument, and learn how to grow a garden. In fact, go back to school when you get a chance, even if you are older, and learn how to keep on learning!

And the most important thing: Make sure to raise someone else up, instead of always yourself. Show your humanity by helping others do better.

That's really the best thing anyone can do—helping others.

Miriam Parker

Dancer & Architect Of Human Space

"Dance is the hidden language of the soul."
-Martha Graham

Lisette: I was bound to meet Miriam in this life, as I expect we've moved through other lives together in the past. I had spent so much of this life with a chip on my shoulder, that my best friend in graduate school aptly described it by saying, "It is at once the most powerful and weakest part of you." By the time I met Miriam, I had transformed that unbalanced power by focusing it on my Dharma practice. A life that had once seemed so haunted by a world that disliked me for my differences, was now itself, different.

The confidence I had gained by sitting opposite the most powerful Civil Rights leaders of our time, walking hand-in-hand with people who had already found power in their differences, and the choice of not being confined to a system (academic, in my case), released me from the prison of the stories that held me bound—I was finally free. "Freedom," as Miriam stated, "is being an individual without being persecuted for it."

It was in that freedom that I threw myself into meditation, yoga and eventually a three-year silent meditation retreat. And it was in that freedom that Miriam found me. I remember when Miriam first took a meditation course from me, and I distinctly remember watching her mind expand right in front of me. She was voracious from the start and has, over the last 12 years, mastered many things along the path. Perhaps it was her upbringing and her focus on play, magic, and joy that inclined her to Buddhism in the first place, but whatever it was, she is indeed a Poderosa in her own right.

Miriam uses dance as a form of protest, as I had used dance as a form of surrender to my culture and my place in it. We have both worked with masters of different forms, in an effort to become better than we ever could have been on our own.

In retreat, I always found that I went the deepest when I stopped pushing towards something and finally just relaxed. That was definitely part of how I found freedom—I stopped pushing and fighting, I put down my dukes, and I dissolved into love. In the end, that sort of surrender is a form of protest, and I expect that Miriam and I have both danced, played, and even fought from the same place, deep in our hearts.

For our conversation, we flew to meet Miriam in her hometown of New York City, where she explained over dinner, and later in a Brooklyn loft, about the deep relationship between dance and the human spirit, perhaps best described here as the movement through time and space.

Miriam, please tell us a little about your development as a dancer, and the evolution of your power. I've witnessed so much of it over the years, but what was it like being born into an artistic family and then finding your voice within it?

Miriam: There was a lot of play in my family, a lot of joy and playfulness. Everything was a game, so there was a lot of joy in that play.

Lisette: How did that manifest, what did it look like?

Miriam: I have different memories of it. One was my own way, which was putting on shows for my family every night. These performances entailed costume changes and interesting uses of clothing, because I have always loved dressing up and the play of costume identity and adornment. I loved looking at fashion, and it became a game for me to figure out how to be in conversation with fashion even when we were dead broke. I was curious how to get to the essence of the trends and build my own interpretations. We couldn't afford to buy anything new, so we'd go to flea markets around town and I'd have about $3.00 to buy stuff. I would come back with a pile of clothes that I would use to embody these different characters. My dad was a big supporter of the art of smart shopping and dressing up.

Mealtime was another space for play, and at that time in my life, from age 7 to 14, I shared my home with many others. We were all together, five girls and one boy, ranging from 0-11-years-old. Everything was play, and in our case, that play bridged worlds from life to death. For example, we would have a live fish in the bathtub—we'd name the fish, talk to it, but then we'd take its life and eat it for dinner.

One of our favorite things was the orchestrated dinner. This was when the matriarch, who was either my mom or Tsana, would play different music, and we had to eat to the music. This was seam-splitting fun! Try eating to the music of Mozart, and then transition to Coltrane, and then Grandmaster Flash. It'd be slow at first, then really fast, and then we'd stop suddenly, so there was this kind of play at mealtime.

Morning time was another place where the play was bright. My dad used to wake me up in the morning by putting things on my toes that were cold and slimy, like pickles or olives. When I was the only one in the house, before the other kids came, he would make pancakes and we would listen to the poetry of Kenneth Patchen—I'm named after his wife, actually. I remember that poetry very clearly, it was the kind of poetry that drew your mind somewhere else.

Another kind of play was when it was warm outside, and we would go on trips to the beach, or the museum, or Central Park. My parents even let us camp outside during a hurricane once, which was really fun. The train would come and we'd run under the turnstiles to avoid the fees. We were living the avant-garde poor life, but we were surrounded by music and dance. There was no rigidity in our family, no real rules, because we were outcasts.

Lisette: Did you know that your family was poor?

Miriam: I knew that we were poor compared to everyone else, like at school—well everyone really. My dad was black and we felt that. I remember wanting to put on white face in 6th grade as a disguise, a strange kind of play at being able to fit in. I'd go to my friend's private school dances, and I learned how to move in those spaces, but I very much wanted to be like everyone else. It felt dangerous to stand out and be raw and unmasked. My mother was raw, and unmasked, and vulnerable and it scared me.

My dad had an upright bass to hide behind (William Parker, the renowned jazz bassist and composer), but my mother is a woman, and she is not of color, however she stood strong in an artistic world that was primarily brown-skinned. She is the grand dame of some other thing, I don't really know how to describe it. Maybe what was scary to me, was her intense belief in the spirit with an invisible inner force, so that when they were performing together it was palpable, it was fleshy. And that scared me, the energy moving between them—I wanted to package that. I was there when they took my Mom to jail for protesting—we went to a lot of protests, but it was scary to see someone go out there like that and get taken to jail. I wanted to protect them.

Lisette: So you grew up in this playful, musical, artistic household, which also held political protest as an important part of life. How did you formalize this into your particular form of dance, and how did you take what you had learned as a child and perfect it into this high art form? It seems like you are expressing joy as a form of political resistance.

Miriam: Yes, but it felt dangerous to me as a child. My parents were doing everything the hard way. They were doing mask work, using masks and strange voices, and they were shaking things and it was scary to me—I didn't like it, so finding my voice within that was hard. One layer was learning to really respect them, another was sitting down, stopping, not reacting to the fear, and just hearing their words, believing in the power of art, and then handing that medicine over to what they were doing. The action of respect, honoring them, holding them—that really helped me to grow.

Lisette: That's beautiful Miriam. Most people never take the time to sit with the things that scare them, nevermind using it to grow and heal. Can you tell us about your formal dance training?

Miriam: My training started when I was about 10-years-old at the Joffrey Ballet, and then at the American School of Ballet. After that I went to LaGuardia Performing Arts High School—it's the actual Fame High School from the movie *Fame*. Then I studied at the Alvin Ailey Dance School, and then the Dance Theatre of Harlem, so on paper I was very Grade A you might say, I did everything right. After high school, I got into Bennington College in Vermont where I studied anthropology and German. I lasted a year before I needed to get back to the fruit of dance, and I didn't understand why people went to college to learn dance.

Returning to New York, I worked with the Jennifer Muller dance company, and from there I went on to Europe to audition for some companies over there. I ended up moving to Amsterdam, where I got into the Ballet Freiburg, and I worked with the famed choreographer, Amanda Miller.

With Amanda's dance troupe, we performed all over the world— Japan, Russia, Thailand, all throughout Europe. I was in Singapore when the World Trade Centers went down on September 11th, and on that same day, we left for the Philippines. It was a strange day, but I knew that my family wouldn't have any reason to be near that area. We performed in the Philippines, and it was gritty—anything Amanda does will take you there. We performed at Philippine military bases, and there was a class of deaf students sitting on the stage, so they could feel the vibration of the live music.

Barrett: That is amazing Miriam. I know there are deaf students who can hear music through their hands and feet, so that would be a profound experience. What was it like returning to New York, after all that global travel and performance? After September 11th, New York must have been a very different city?

Miriam: Well, I was still living in Europe at the time, and we were on tour in Southeast Asia when it happened. We went on to Bangkok after the Philippine shows, so my first reaction to the World Trade Center was concern for my immediate family, although I knew they wouldn't be anywhere near the towers. But I honestly wasn't that surprised about it either, what with our cocky American colonial attitude, so honestly, it didn't change a lot for me. I am not particularly proud about this, but there is a power to transform people during a large disaster when it happens to a collective group.

Barrett: I was in a recording studio in Seattle on September 11th and I thought the same thing—it was horrific, but it was also the result of our foreign policies in the Middle East, coming back to haunt us. But when we played in New York in 2002, it was beautiful to see how New Yorkers had healed and rebounded. You could feel a deeper wisdom in the city—they were survivors.

Miriam: Yep, New Yorkers are a tough, resilient people.

Lisette: How did the experience of being in different dance companies in both the US and Europe influence your individual and spontaneous dance style? How was that received in other countries where you danced?

Miriam: It was always there. Even within the choreography of these other companies, there was always a spine of my individuality in there. What was very influential, however, was working with Amanda and her Bauhaus influence, which uses the nine-points system of movement. I began to understand the mechanics of these shapes, and how to move within them. Amanda was more about being in constant movement and never stopping, which is a kind of tipping point—it was all tipping and spirals.

Lisette: How many dancers would be in a travelling dance troupe like that?

Miriam: About 10 dancers total. And we had an amazing studio in Germany with windows looking out over the Black Forest. I danced with Amanda's company for two years, and then I returned for an additional year. I also got into studying the architecture of Le Corbusier and Frank Lloyd Wright, the phenomenology of perception, and artists like Richard Serra and Agnes Martin. It was a moment of real mental and heart opening for me.

Lisette: I've seen Agnes Martin's paintings, they are simple yet profoundly elegant. It's amazing to see the evolution of a great artist as they get older and their art changes over time. What did you learn about the connection between painting, traditional architecture, and the architecture of dance as you developed as a dancer?

Miriam: All architecture is about creating space for things to take place within it, whether it's life, family—really everything. And that is what dance is.

Barrett: I can totally see that, because we use music and dance to create sacred space, and in our ancient past, we banged the bones of ancestors together to bring their spirits back into that space. In some cultures, the word for music is literally the same word for dance—it's the same thing.

Miriam: They are one and the same, music and dance, there is no spearation between the two.

Lisette: So you came back from Europe with all this formal dance training and a lot of international touring experience. You brought all of those ideas back to New York City—how did that inform your individual style of dance?

Miriam: I started working on a lot of solo material, including my relationship to the stage. I wanted to be invisible, finding the tension between wanting to feel safe, but also extending myself out into space. How can you be in these two places at once? You create bridges to toggle between those spaces. That bridge becomes a kind of wonderment, like a portal. It's that clear view of the water, and the clear view of the mind holding that water.

Lisette: How did you know that dancing would be your form of expression, rather than say, music, like your father?

Miriam: It was never a question—I was always a dancer, and I've been dancing for as long as I can remember. I love to be silly, and I love to move my body and dance. I was around dance all the time, it started in my mother's womb, and she never had a babysitter, so I was with her at all her shows. I was also very quiet as a child, so I could hold that quietness. There are stories of me falling asleep inside the bass drum—I could just go there and be still.

My father is very good at that connection between silence and music, in a very specific way. The first book he gave me was *The Bhagavad*

Gita, and I don't think that was when I actually read it, but it was the first book he gave me. He wrote me letters on my birthdays, and he would write about purpose through the perspective of Native American cultures. He would explain how, in their villages, there was always a healer, a teacher, a warrior, and everyone made art, so there was a place for everyone. I would remember his letters more as I got older—he's a beautiful writer, but he doesn't speak very much. His letters were always about having confidence in the power of creative expression, and his letters were there to empower me. Always the message was, dance is powerful, music is powerful, and it can change the world.

My father has this unfailing clarity and concreteness about his purpose—it is unshakable. I would have conversations with him about fame, and how do you reconcile not getting recognition? He would just say, "You don't really understand how this works. There might only be three people in the audience, but they are as important as three hundred people." And through these conversations with him, I learned how to grow into my own power. I would ask, is this true? And if it is true, then how do I play with this truth?

For a while, the play was me holding this precious thing that I thought was happening outside of me, but I didn't have the clarity of mind that my father had. When I looked at the great actors and great dancers of the world, I would try to imitate them, but that was not giving me the essence of what I wanted either. Yes, I got the best scholarships, I got the best jobs, I was always cast, but I was not satisfied at all. I didn't know how to do it, but I could see it, and I just had to take care of that vision.

Lisette: Was there a linchpin moment that helped you turn that corner and make it your own, to become that personal vision?

Miriam: I think there were many linchpins. There was my own experience and love for the craft, and watching myself figure it all out. Deciding not to dance, at one point, was actually very empowering for me, and not giving up. I remember sitting in the studio with Jo— she's my mom's best friend, and she is a visual artist and painter. We started collaborating in 2010, when I went to work with her on our first interactive installation together, and we were stuck. So I just sat there looking at this tree that was in the middle of the installation—I just stared at that tree until I knew what to do. I just had to wish it to be.

When I started practicing the Dharma—that was a huge thing. I was listening to Buddhist teachers speak, and around the same time, I also had the experience of going into hell when I accidentally set my nightgown on fire and burned my arm terribly.

Lisette: How did you find your way back to dance after the experience of burning your arm?

Miriam: It was like a pilot light that was still on, and my whole youth was about something I wasn't able to understand yet, but it was my light that I had to hold on to. So I offered myself as much as I could to my teachers. I had been in Israel suffering through a terrible relationship, which was really me and my own demons, so I eventually left my partner, and I left Israel. I got really clean and healthy and tried to find myself again. I wondered, could I design a space in which I could truly move? I couldn't use my body at that point, so I decided to work with space. I was trying to create a kind of altar for my body to rest on, and I realized that I was already working through the body, but there was still some stigma I was holding on to, where the female body was not respected. I felt a great comfort in working this way.

Lisette: It's like your parents had been teaching you Tantra (secret Buddhist teachings) ever since you were born.

Miriam: I studied their teachings, and the first question I asked out loud was, I see paradise all around me, but I can't get there. I still didn't want to be seen as a dancer, it didn't feel like it held all of me. I was still working through shame and lots of doubt, and that's when I decided to really work on the love and respect for my mother. I also decided that I needed to learn how to transform things, so if you're not feeling that you're beautiful, that's just not OK. I didn't feel beautiful at that point, so I had to do the work to feel beautiful again.

Lisette: And the short films you are now making—are those bridges too?

Miriam: Oh yeah, oh yeah! The stillness in the dance is also a bridge. It's interesting, because this is why I like plastic forms and sculpture, it's looking for a position within space. Now I'm looking at the frame itself, and that's a portal too—to be still enough, to work with paint on the human body, to re-frame the body, and to place it in between the sculpture, the myth, and the archetype. And I'm working on expanding my vocabulary of how to create that offering to others in a physical space, where they can move into it as well. Erecting spaces for refuge is a very important thing for me as well.

Lisette: Is the little girl looking for safety and wanting to share it?

Miriam: Oh yes, of course.

Lisette: Is the path of dance—does it restart every time? Is it facing your fear every time you dance? Does it feel like that?

Miriam: I wouldn't say every time, but there are always lessons for me to learn. For example, I was recently in a meditation retreat and my body was totally breaking down. I was fainting, I was confused, and I was not moving very much. When I dance, I barely warm up my body, and I look at the space inside of me and I just hit the stage. I look for the places of discomfort and I stay there, allowing people to see that, and I allow them to go there with me if they so wish. Allowing them to see that—that's real power. To me, it feels more like an offering.

Lisette: I like how that energy reveals itself, it's always about space, or trust, or a kind of power and prayer. And the energy in the modern world has swung so far to the masculine, that we now have to chip it back so we can find the center again. How does dance teach that balance?

Miriam: That is the real magic, and what is happening in my work now, is that I am looking at the journey of self-expression, as pieces of the mystery. How can I pull these disparate pieces together, how can I manifest and bring it to life, and then share it with the world? It's the process of trying to create an organic form, of placing myself inside of that organism, to find the stillness in that. Do not kill it by knowing it, because if you think you know it, then you really don't know it!

Aristotle's definition of creativity is something that has to be given over to another person, meaning that it is not an exhibit of something, but rather it is an unveiling of something that wouldn't exist unless another person is partaking in it. You can't control what people think, but people can feel when you are open to them—they can feel your integrity, and the letting go of trying so hard. That keeps bringing me back to the body, and specifically to place the female body in a space that is a form of protest.

A body that is not white is also important, because it's a personal thing for me. There were times when I wasn't allowed into the galleries—I was only allowed to be a thing I didn't even think I was. Now it feels like a form of protest because I'm saying, "I am here now, and I want to be here, now."

Barrett: I totally understand that architecture of music and your definition of space, because I worked with an Indigenous dance company called Dancing Earth in Santa Fe, NM. They had both men and women, but it was led by an incredible female choreographer named Rulan Tangen. I would observe their rehearsals and then compose rhythms that worked with their movements—it was symbiotic, the interplay between rhythm and movement. Their themes were very organic, and it would be things like a seed that germinated and became an entire forest, or the elements of water and fire moving through the body and across the Earth. How did growing up in New York City help you interpret that space, which I presume would be more of an urban space?

Miriam: I love that you're asking me this! I spent a lot of time looking out the window of our apartment as a child—a lot of time. On my dad's first album, *Through Acceptance Of The Mystery Of Peace*, I'm on the back cover looking out of our window. I would look out that window and I would see the fire escapes—that jungle gym of horizontal and vertical lines, and I would be moving along those lines. So my interpretation of space is very geometrical, it was based on that grid, and the first piece I made with Jo was a scrim with grid lines, threaded through metal bars.

Also, there is great confrontation between live, moving human bodies, versus a still painting, or a figure behind a pixelated *Tulle* scrim, when the body becomes two dimensional and easier to examine.

Lisette: I've noticed that with a lot of new modern dance, particularly when there is an influence like hip hop, those kinds of urban styles are being absorbed across a wide range of choreography. It seems, from my observations, that modern dancers on the popular stage are starting to embody a hybrid of organic body movements, which the Indigenous dancers naturally possess, mixed with a more urban influence, which is a harder and edgier form of dance from the cities. I see this as highly shamanic, even anthropomorphic in the way they integrate these divergent styles. Can you describe this evolution in modern dance, the way you see it?

Miriam: I saw the merger between traditional ballet and street dance in the work of William Forsythe and his nine-point system. This is about dividing space and the body, where you occupy the center, but you become very aware of the architecture and manipulation of space.

And there are a lot of new ideas emerging from this right now, like how you imagine water dripping from your palms as you move, or you imagine your bones are made of ice. How would you move if your bones were made of ice? Or what if your body was made of spaghetti, spaghetti, spaghetti! (wiggling her arms like spaghetti noodles) So you move like you're made of spaghetti. I dance like that a lot.

Lisette: That is so cool Miriam! And this is obviously why you can't choreograph your dances—you perform them freely, much like your dad's free jazz music.

Miriam: Well, my dad's music is not unchoreographed, nor is my movement, because it takes great choreographic sense to become a conduit for things to move through you like that. It is the holding of stillness that creates the movement, that creates the flow, and the flow gives room for new discovery, which is the healing aspect of dance.

Lisette: In that stillness, in that flow of the dance you're channeling, what is the energy you feel moving through your body?

Miriam: It's a kind of medicine. Because dance has been incredibly powerful as a form of healing for me, which is ultimately what this is all about.

Because dancing is really about healing.

Erin Currier

Artist, Writer & Activist

"You have to act as if it were possible to radically transform the world.
And then you have to do it all the time."

–Angela Davis

Lisette: Barrett, you've known Erin Currier for almost 25 years, and you have witnessed first-hand her remarkable artistic evolution. Can you introduce her to all of us, as we set up this final story of the book?

Barrett: I first met Erin Currier and her late partner, Anthony Hassett, in 1996 when I was visiting mutual friends in Taos, New Mexico. All of us went on a hike together in the magnificent Sangre de Cristo Mountains, in the high desert of northern New Mexico. We all had much in common—a great love of music, art, and an obscure martial art that we were studying with the same master in Taos. Even though we were all relatively young, we seemed to understand each other in a deeper way that old souls recgonize in each other.

Now almost 25 years later, much has happened. We lost Anthony to cancer three years ago, just as he was beginning to express his extraordinary literary and visual art talent, which people are finally appreciating today. Erin also continued to grow in those years, almost exponentially, to the degree that her own artwork has been featured in museums and collections around the United States, Europe, and South America. Five books of her paintings and writings have been published so far, including a monograph, and her art work has graced the covers of numerous magazines, albums, and other people's books, including the cover for this one, *Poderosas*. If you look at this book cover long enough, you'll see that everything Erin describes about her art is revealed in the painting.

Erin's art is based around the portrait tradition, but her work is unlike any portraits you've ever seen. Her subjects are human rights activists, educators, laborers, poets, musicians, athletes, and other heroic figures, most of whom are unknown, including some who have been martyred. Many of them are people Erin and Tony met in their travels around the world, to countries and environments that very few travelers ever visit. By immortalizing these unknown people, from shoeshine boys, to the women who maintain lavatories in the Global South, Erin has changed the way we see people by focusing on their faces. In doing so, she makes everyone appear like a holy being, as someone sacred and worthy of equal respect. Having known Erin for so many years, I have seen her work progress into something truly extraordinary in the world of art, which is why her reputation now precedes her in art circles around the world.

Lisette: We spoke with Erin over the course of two days, after we flew to her home in New Mexico, almost exactly two years from the date of Anthony's passing. Erin picked us up at the Albuquerque Sunport in her new Toyota pickup truck, and as we sped across the New Mexico desert, our conversation began in classic, road trip style, which continued over dinner at our favorite Mexican restaurant in Santa Fe.

Erin, in 1996 you and Tony had just gotten together as a couple, and not long after that, you had your first solo art exhibit in Taos, at a coffee shop called *The Bean*. Can you please tell us how that all came together?

Erin: Well, I had just gotten my BFA from the College of Santa Fe theatre department, and Tony and I had moved to Taos, where I got a job working as a barista and waiting tables at *The Bean*. I was blown away by the amount of trash that was being thrown out every day, so I started gathering all the trash at the end of my shifts and transforming the debris into Buddhist deities. I had also been doing a lot of Tibetan Bon meditation at the time, and learning how to do Buddhist *Thangka* paintings.

I had my first solo show at *The Bean* in 1998, and it was a great success. It was on the radio, on the front page of the newspaper, I sold most of the work, and I received a lot of positive feedback. Viewers were able to see the statement I was making in regards to impermanence and transformation. Then I was picked up by a couple of galleries—one in Taos and one in Malibu, and soon after that, I was able to quit the barista job, and work full-time as an artist.

Barrett: I remember having a dinner party at my house in Taos and you said you had decided to dedicate yourself to art full-time—it was like a command to the universe, and apparently the universe listened! I said, right then and there, that I wanted to commission three pieces from you: a Manjushri and two Sarasvati paintings, so I asked you how much for all three, and I wrote a check on the spot. I still have two of those paintings, and that was the first time I ever commissioned an artist. You said, if I remember correctly, that was also your first direct commission.

Erin: It was actually, and it was also around the same time that I began exhibiting at the Parks Gallery in Taos, and the Tops Gallery in Malibu. Between those two galleries, they were able to sell all of my early works. I was also doing murals, antique finishes, and decorative painting in Taos and Santa Fe, so I was able to work full-time as an artist by the early part of 2000—the beginning of the new millennium.

Lisette: And you have done an annual show ever since?

Erin: Yes, beginning in 1998, I've done a gallery show every year for 22 years. Sometimes I have 2-3 additional shows, in places like Buenos Aires, Berlin, or Venice Beach. In the past two years, I also had my first major museum retrospective.

Lisette: What inspired you to use the Buddhist Thangka painting technique, and how did that evolve into some of the more European influences that are now appearing in your art?

Erin: I think my work has both Eastern and Modernist influences, in addition to being deeply inspired by Latin American Art, especially that of the Mexican muralist, Diego Rivera. It is a long historical trajectory, but basically I was painting Buddhist deities and doing my daily spiritual practice, and in that practice, I envisioned these deities as embodiments of compassion and wisdom. I had an epiphany that this is all fine and good, to visualize these ancient deities with all of these positive attributes, but where are the living examples of it in the world today?

Simultaneously, I had become interested in the Civil Rights Movement, and had begun reading a lot about it in books such as Taylor Branch's *Parting The Waters,* and it just totally blew my mind. That's where I found embodiments of the Bodhisattvas in our world today, in the Civil Rights activists who were dedicating their lives to equality and human dignity.

I started creating portraits of Civil Rights activists depicted as Buddhist deities, like Septima Clark, who taught thousands of people how to read and write, who I painted as Prajnaparamita, the goddess of wisdom. I also painted Angela Davis as the Green Tara, and Bob Moses as the Medicine Buddha, just as some examples.

At the same time, I was able to save money to travel the world, something I had yearned to do for as long as I could remember. Anthony and I took our first nine-month trip around the world—it blew my mind for several reasons.

First, I saw that the struggle for human rights was not just relegated to the US, but that it was a worldwide event, and that there were similar struggles happening everywhere. I was also profoundly affected by the economic disparity I saw, but I also saw how warm and kind people are, how much the same we all are, and the commonalities we share. I experienced that most people are good, and their needs are basic and universal: a roof over their head, to be of service in their communities, to raise a family, eat good food, and have access to clean water.

So my work kept shifting and became more humanist, more narrative, and based on social justice and transformation. But I never looked at it as being solely political or solely spiritual—I looked at the spiritual and the political as being one and the same. It's the same internal battle to overcome anger and desire, played out on the world stage. The underlying foundation of all of my work is an expression of respect for all sentient beings.

Barrett: When you started taking those trips with Tony, you'd both be gone for almost a year at a time. You lived in Kathmandu, Bangkok, Rome, Berlin, and Buenos Aires for extended periods of time, and you were also exposed to human rights activists and spiritual teachers that Americans are almost never made aware of. Those people, plus all the trash you brought back from those countries, found their way into your art as a kind of global, collage-montage. Can you describe your collage technique, because it's so unique to your style?

Erin: I always keep travel journals, and I gather post-consumer waste the entire time I am traveling. Every portrait I create is comprised of trash from all over the world, and I like to find packaging in as many languages, and with as many cultural references as possible. This makes the statement that the emancipatory struggle is an international one, thereby highlighting our commonalities in every piece I create.

I consider myself to be more of a traveling ontographer, documenting the environments that I encounter, and incorporating discarded ephemera from the streets into portraits of figures who resist or defy authority, as well as people who live outside of their societal conventions. The discarded waste becomes re-transfigured into something beautiful, in the same way that discarded human beings—like women who clean bathrooms, and men who shine shoes, are recognized on the same platform as oil barons and kings.

Lisette: Those street sweepers, the *lustrabotas* and *obreros,* are examples of people that Americans wouldn't be exposed to unless they were global travelers, which is not common. What is the process by which you find these people? Is it research, or local people telling you about them? I'm particularly interested in your subjects from Southeast Asia and the Middle East, as I have a particular fondness for those parts of the world. I fear that many Americans would know very little about them, and most couldn't point to those countries on a map, yet here are all these great humanitarians from those countries. Many are born from the hardships created by the bombs that we decided to drop on them.

Erin: Well, I immerse myself in the daily life of countries I visit, studying languages, getting around on foot or by bus, sketching, documenting, making friends, and collecting trash. Sometimes I read about someone, sometimes I'll hear a story or encounter someone directly, like Leila, who cleans bathrooms by the Sphinx in Egypt, for example. Often, one person will lead me to the next.

For example, when I was in the process of researching poets and revolutionaries in Nicaragua, I came upon a small museum founded by the mothers of slain Sandinistas. I spoke with one of the mothers, an openhearted woman named Juana, and I became inspired to portray the mothers themselves. She loaned me some photographs, which I copied at a print shop and then returned to her.

On another occasion, Anthony and I were traveling in Southeast Asia on the border between Laos and Thailand, and we kept seeing a man's face on the telephone poles. He had this beautiful, warm face, so we began asking the local people about him, and we found out that his name was Sombath Somphone and that he had been disappeared by the police because he was a humanitarian and thus, a threat to their power. It was feared that they had murdered him, so I did a portrait of him as the Buddha.

Lisette: You grew up with somewhat of a social justice background— did you begin to feel that drive within yourself as you grew into your artistic expression?

Erin: Yes, my parents actually met at an Abby Hoffman rally in the late 1960s! (everyone laughs)

My mother protested against a factory that was polluting a local river—there is a photo from the front page of a local newspaper with her holding my baby sister and looking indignant. One of my aunts was arrested for storming the fence at the Seabrook Nuclear Power Plant.

Another thing I admired about my mother, is she had this little book called, *Shopping For a Better World,* and she would always bring it to the grocery store. My sister and I would want some cookies or some juice and she'd look up the product's company and say, "Nope, we can't buy that because they don't hire women for a fair wage," or they test on animals, or that company doesn't have any people of color in executive positions.

Lisette: I love that, it's really the first level of the divest and boycott movement against predatory corporations and oppressive countries that abuse their own people. It's making a comeback now, and social media is the new version of that little book your mom carried to the grocery store.

Erin: Well, it was frustrating for a 6-year-old, but even back then I knew my mother was right. I didn't want to eat something from a place that was polluting the environment, or discriminating against people based on their gender or ethnicity. My parents instilled in me a real ethical core, for which I am grateful.

Lisette: If you were in an alternate universe, if you hadn't met Tony, would you still have traveled so much?

Erin: Oh absolutely! Growing up, I couldn't wait to travel. I had a map of the world, and I would stare at it and try to imagine daily life in all the various countries. I begged my parents, "Can we go to China or Japan?" As I got older, geography was the one class where I got an A++, I just loved it! Any time one of our family friends would come back from another country, I would just grill them about everything they saw. I couldn't wait to get out in the world, so as soon as I turned 18 and graduated from high school, I left New England to drive across the US.

I had been accepted to a number of East Coast art schools, and I was even offered scholarships, but I wanted to see the world. In truth, I wanted to be a screenwriter and a costume designer, so I enrolled at the College of Santa Fe, which had a great theatre department.

Lisette: You've been a professional artist for over 20 years now, and your work is in galleries around the US, Europe, South America, and increasingly collected by museums. You've also been speaking and lecturing, and writing essays, which are beautifully written and reflective of your philosophy. The social justice message is more apparent now than ever, and it's causing young people to become aware of the products they buy. Can you describe how you navigate this new position, as an artist who is both speaking and publishing? And what is the role of the artist in the world we now live in?

Erin: I think everyone has a role in the potential transformation of our world, and I feel that art is an important piece of that. If nothing else, but for the active-imagining power of art, because there is less and less of that in our contemporary world.

When we first traveled the world, the Internet had just started and it was few and far between to find an Internet cafe to email our family and friends. Tony and I traveled for days and weeks at a time without any contact. We didn't know where we were going, and this was before every inch of the world was made accessible by the swipe of a finger. There were guidebooks, but these were extremely limited, and entire towns were absent from them, so most of where we visited was via word of mouth. We'd have to ask around to figure out which train to jump on, or where to find a boat. That process fueled our imaginations.

Staring at that world map as a kid, imagining all those possibilities, what the world was like, what people were like, how they communicated—that's the danger of smartphones and social media, losing the sublime mystery of it all. But this could all shift again, everything is possible.

Lisette: How did you develop this powerful philosophy on life, and the way it is represented in your art and writing?

Erin: With ancient Indigenous civilizations, they had infinite modes of being, and infinite ways of structuring a society—autonomous, self-governing societies. As a species, we need to collectively see that this particular globalized reality is not how it has to be, that there are other ways we can live. Often people feel stuck or become intractable, but that's where art comes into play. And travel too—it presents different ways of seeing and being.

For example, if you get a group of artists in one room drawing the same subject, you'll end up with as many variations in drawings as there are artists in the room. This is why counter-power, rooted in imagination, is crucial. There is no single way to attain liberation, each method must be appropriate to the situation, utilizing the information and tools available at the time.

Here's another example: In 17th Century England, sowing the ground with parsnips, carrots, and beans was considered to be an act of treason! It was a revolutionary action of the diggers and gardeners, who had been impoverished by England's sudden and arbitrary process of privatizing The Commons. This act was the digger's means by which to alleviate hunger and free themselves from servitude and slavery. They felt that this freedom to the common Earth was a poor person's right, by the Law Of Creation.

Barrett: That's a perfect example of an unjust law, written by unjust men, being challenged by the righteous. It's the responsibility of enlightened people to break those kinds of laws, like Ghandi making salt from the Arabian Sea, or the Freedom Riders of the Civil Rights Movement, or an American soldier refusing to follow an illegal order—it's immoral, therefore it's not a legitimate order.

Erin: Exactly, and guerilla gardening is an effective act of resistance to this day. The Black Panthers occupying the statehouse was another, or factory workers occupying and running defunct factories in Argentina is another example. Most recently, the nonviolent methods of the Water Protectors at Standing Rock in North Dakota, chaining themselves to bulldozers, linking arms, crawling inside pipes, has had unprecedented reverberations throughout the world. It succeeded in galvanizing Indigenous people across hundreds of tribes, as well as people all over the US and the world.

Lisette: This period you are in now, where you take Classic and Modernist paintings and reimagine them with Indigenous faces in non-European environments—what inspired this? Because so much European and American art didn't include Indigenous people, unless they were depicted as the noble savage, which is the farthest thing from the truth. The Indigenous people were far more socially advanced than Europeans or Americans, and the Native Americans already had democracy in the League Of The Iroquois, whereas the Europeans and early Americans were still subjects of various brutal monarchies.

Erin: My new series pays homage to Classical and Modernist masterpieces, while addressing contemporary issues that have compelled my work. So I'm focusing on Immigrant's Rights, Worker's Rights, Women's Rights, Civil Rights, and basic human dignity. For example, Eugene Delacroix's epic painting, *Liberty Leading the People,* provides the composition and palette for a painting I did that portrays Indigenous women on both sides of the US/Mexico border, dismantling the border wall. In my rendition, feminine strength and grace in action, is in the form of Indigenous women.

All of the works in my new series are grounded in a feminine focal point. For example, in another painting, I depict United Farm Workers co-founder and activist, Dolores Huerta, replacing the male gardener in an homage to Vincent Van Gogh's, *The Gardener.* So the women step into the foreground, not as passive subjects, but as fully engaged and active participants. The emancipatory moment is right now, so for me as an artist, now is the time to honor those who came before me.

Barrett: You grew up in a small New England town that was mostly White people, and I grew up in an equally small town that was mostly White. It occurred to me that until you leave those places and start exploring your own ideas and other cultures, you don't really learn anything about the world. If you stay in rural, White America, it's very limited in what you can learn, and you become unable to comprehend all the other cultures around the world. Your art allows another person who hasn't traveled very much to get a glimpse of the larger world through your eyes, and that's a pretty remarkable thing to convey, because only a very accomplished artist can do that—teaching through their art form.

Erin: I try to portray people from all over the world. However, when I travel to a particular place, I allow the people and culture of that place to take precedent in my work. My most recent show focused on people from Bali, Australia, Peru and Mexico. And as far as the teaching modality in my work, I'm trying to bring back knowledge that I acquired on those specific journeys. I talk with lots of people in the places I have been to, in order to get a sense of what their day-to-day existence is like.

Lisette: And probably a lot of conversations about our similarities too? Your mom's influence was socially very forward-thinking.

Erin: That's very true. I recently heard Boots Riley speak, and I loved that he tied everything back to economic disparity and class struggle, because really, if you are economically oppressed, then it doesn't matter how many rights you have on paper. If you cannot afford a roof over your head, to put food on the table for your children, to have access to clean water, to have a dignified life that every human being deserves, then these are all forms of oppression.

Lisette: And that's exactly what Martin Luther King was starting to focus on in his marches. He was beginning to lead protests against economic inequality across all races, and that's when they assassinated him. He had realized the trick the US government was using against everyone—they were playing the races against each other, when it was really about economic inequality *within* the races. He saw that it was about class division, as much as racial division.

Erin: Absolutely, and the economic disparity has only worsened since MLK's time. I just read an econmic report where eight men control more than 50% of the world's wealth and resources—they own the equivalent of what the rest of us seven billion people share. It's obscene.

Lisette: The best description I've heard on the role of the artist, is that it is their job to take the complexities of a given society, and reinterpret those complexities in such a manner that the average person can understand what is really happening in their society. This includes race, economic class, spiritual and cultural beliefs—pretty much everything. How do you convey all of those things, through the medium of your art?

Erin: That's what I love about utilizing trash in my art—the post consumer waste comments further on the story of the subjects I paint. I am able to include humor and cultural references through the use of the ephemera, which makes it a multilayered tapestry.

For example, that painting where I depict Native American women dismantling the border wall on both sides of the US/Mexico border—for that piece, I used a ticket from a Frida Kahlo photography exhibition, with a photo of Frida looking in the mirror, reflected back on herself. I collaged it into the border wall of the painting, thus making the statement that we are seeing ourselves reflected. You take down a border and the people on the other side are essentially you.

The use of trash also allows for people to make their own references. For example, I have a Czech friend who noticed that a word on a Czech political poster I had used in a painting meant, *change*. And I used a torn Arabic poster from Lebanon that turned out to say, *transformation is in your hands*. I love how the viewer's perspective adds to each piece.

Lisette: The last time we spoke, you talked about how stepping into your power meant having the courage to destroy a perfectly painted portrait in order to do the trash collage over the top. I love that—can you describe that process a little more?

Erin: The process is very much like a spiritual practice for me, in that I draw the painting first, and then I paint it. At that point, I have this completed painting that I am happy with, and then I have to glue all of this ephemera all over it. I never know if I will be able to bring it back to life from beneath the trash. It's really a process of letting go and trusting.

Barrett: Well, I've seen you go through that process many times over the years, and you've gotten really good at it. A comment about the use of humor in your art: I've seen dozens of your paintings, and a lot of the trash you use is printed with funny anecdotes, innuendos, and double entendres. So even with a political or spiritual message, there can be a sense of humor, even if it is about someone who has been assassinated, or martyred by a government or right wing death squad. You are able to show the beauty and humor in their lives.

Lisette: Exactly, because Western historical art is so full of violence. If you go to the Louvre, or the Vatican, or any traditional museum, the paintings are mostly White men in battle, on horses, trampling other people of color, and cutting them down with swords. A lot of the victims are Indigenous people. There is absolutely no humor to be found in any of those places, it's mostly just violence and religious guilt. How do you find the joy and humor in the subjects of your paintings? Was Tony a big part of that?

Erin: Anthony was the funniest guy in the world, and everyone who ever met him said that. I used to say to him that if I were in prison or in solitary confinement, the only thing I would want is to be able to laugh. Laughing means more than even a meal. It's the greatest gift to laugh, and it is how he won my heart, why I fell in love with him.

So yes, I try to bring that humor into my work, because there is already so much darkness, violence, and cruelty in the world, although I do believe that most people are essentially good. But there is an element out there that is very, very dark, the same forces that have allowed a situation in which eight white men control half of the world's resources.

I've found that I can bring a little light to the world through my work, painting people who are uplifting and inspiring. And my hope is that when I am dealing with a dark subject matter, like the assassination of a Yemini schoolboy, or the Alabama church bombing that killed four young girls, then I can say that there are some things that cannot be destroyed—the spirit that persists beyond the body, social movements that span across lifetimes, and even love itself. It's like what the Black Panther Fred Hampton said, "You can kill the revolutionary, but you can't kill the revolution."

Barrett: Or Martin Luther King Jr., "The arc of the universe is long, but it bends toward justice."

Lisette: You were recently an artist in residence in Joshua Tree, CA, where there is a huge artistic enclave. The artists and musicians are leaving Los Angeles, and American cities in general. It's being called the *Hipsturbia* movement. Artists are leaving cities and moving to the suburbs, and even out to the country, because the cities have become unaffordable places for people to create. They can't afford the space needed to do their work, especially artists who need space and light, and they have been priced out. This is also, ironically, going to change the political demographics, because all these educated and cosmopolitan creative people are moving to places that were traditionally more conservative.

Erin: Yes, it's really interesting how society follows the artists. Wherever they go, everyone else follows.

Barrett: Artists seek out the old, forgotten places and make them cool again, and then all the technology and urban professionals follow in their footsteps, inevitably ruining the fun. It's exactly what happened to San Francisco and Seattle—the art and music scenes were decimated by the technology companies who exploited those areas and made them unaffordable.

I always thought it was interesting how artists and musicians are respected and revered after they get to a certain point in their career, the point of fame and so-called success. But American society doesn't really respect them throughout this long process, or allow them the time and space to do their work when they are young and vital. I've often wondered what that disconnect is? I expect these are the toxic tailings of capitalism, because the opposite is true with Indigenous societies—they revere their artists and musicians.

Erin: Yes, totally! The profit-driven capitalist mentality is parasitizing the entire planet.

Lisette: And it has really metastasized lately!

Erin: Unfettered capitalism undermines kindness, sharing, dignity, respect for the planet, and respect for the arts and the artists who create them. For example, if a person has a great loft space with lots of light, our capitalist system conditions and even encourages the property owner to rent it to a stockbroker for ten times what they could rent it to an aspiring musician, or an artist, or a student, or a young family starting out, or even a retired senior citizen. On an individual level, we have these choices. Do we just take all the money we can possibly get, or is it more important that we connect with one another and support our fellow human beings?

If you own a restaurant, do you want it filled with students and working class folks, with artists and elderly people who just want a good, affordable meal? Or do you want to jack up the prices up so that only the elites can go there? Unfortunately, with the privatization of so many of our institutions, like schools, prisons, hospitals—money is valued more than education, health, well-being, or even dignity.

Lisette: In most Indigenous cultures, there is no separate word for art. Their creations are in their weavings, beadwork, it's on their clothing, on their pottery, on their homes, and on their bodies. Art is not a separate part of life for them, and their art is not rarified and commodified into a thing to sell—unless they choose to sell it.

When I was a kid, it seemed like everybody played a musical instrument, made their clothes, painted, and made artwork for the family business or restaurant. Where did that all go? I see it when we travel to remote areas of the world, but not as much in American cities.

Erin: Art remains alive and well all over the world. Artists find beauty in places that are run down and forgotten. In Detroit, where the city had been abandoned and was rife with vacant lots and crumbling buildings, the artists took them over. Guerilla gardeners planted gardens in vacant lots, and homeless mothers and their children created safe, clean, sustainable homes within the abandoned houses. It's the perfect metaphor for what we were discussing earlier, which is the transformative power of art. The artist comes along and transforms the rundown place into a treasure, like what is happening in the Salton Sea area now, and then everyone is able to see this hidden jewel and say, hey I want to live there too!

Barrett: That's true, the artists and musicians do most of the work transforming a place, but then are pushed out once the property values go up—again, capitalism at its worst. But I agree, this is a very true dynamic, how the artistic class can transform the canvas, or the abandoned building, or an entire city into something more beautiful.

How do we use that to awaken people about more looming things, like political extremism, economic inequality, or the very dangerous climate crisis, all of which are closely related? I think we will be contending with these issues for a very long time, probably into the next century.

Erin: Well, if you really want to know what I think (laughing), I think that all borders, and governments, and militaries should be dismantled. This colonial, imperial experiment has run its course, it has failed miserably, and it has become parasitic and brought the world to the brink of destruction. All occupied lands should be given back to the Indigenous people, to the extent that they become custodians of the land again.

Lands, waters, and all resources for that matter, should never be owned by any corporation, so it is our responsibility as human beings to take care of the Earth. We are inextricably connected to it, and Indigenous people have known this for thousands of years. They lived in perfect harmony with their environments, so their rightful place is at the vanguard of the future, and the rest of us must support them.

Lisette: We totally agree! The Indigenous people have tens of thousands of years of observational experience in their environments, whereas we've only been on this continent for about 500 years and all we've done is destroy the environment.

Erin: But even we as artists, who try to live outside of it as much as possible—we are also complicit in this, because we live and work within this uber-structure. Fortunately, a lot of conscious people are trying to break out of it.

Barrett: Agreed, we're in the system too, and it's parallel to working for the old company store model. That's when the only employment is with one company, you're paid with money printed on company paper with an arbitrary value, and you have to buy everything at the company store at exorbitant prices—and you're always in debt to them. They designed the system to enslave you, without you even knowing you were enslaved.

The Brazilian rubber barons did this to their workers, the American fruit and coffee companies did it to their Latin American workers, as did the American timber companies, where my great-grandparents worked for the company store, using money that was worthless paper outside of the logging camps. This is essentially the world we are forced to live in, and I mean very literally—it's going in that direction.

We should be buying and harvesting our food from local farmers, and using new modes of distribution that benefit people at the local level, rather than the corporate. We are all complicit in this fossil fuel environmental destruction, but we were born into it, so it was all we knew. But the more we wake up and become self-aware, the more power the people have, and this is especially true with the power of the purse—that is where we can be extremely effective.

Lisette: Right, and you know, the old revolution models just don't work anymore, and violence has never worked except to oppress others, so it has to be peaceful and nonviolent, with a focused intention on the people's financial power—kind of like that book your mom used to take to the grocery store. Who will we vote for, or against? Which products will we buy, or not? The artist makes this societal awakening into a visible, audible, understandable thing.

Barrett: I read this quote by Stanley Kubrick, where he said that saying something directly to the audience does not have nearly as much power as when you tell the story with integrity and subtlety. When you let the viewer become engaged with the deeper message, it has much more of an impact on them. So we can say that building a wall on the

Mexico border is absurd, because anyone who has read history or visited that border, knows that it will always come down, and the only people who will benefit is the corporation who builds it—temporarily.

Lisette: Right, and when Erin painted that portrait showing Indigenous women with babies on their backs, dismantling the border wall, that has real power behind it. The symbolic references that enter the mind are far more effective with that kind of powerful imagery, much more then any words could convey.

Erin: Yes, the visual effect is extremely powerful, and that's why our government wouldn't allow photographs of the dead soldiers coming back from Afghanistan and Iraq. During the Vietnam War, people actually saw the dead soldiers coming home every night on the news, and it sparked all the protests and direct action by the people, which eventually led to the end of the Vietnam War.

Barrett: I remember seeing the Vietnam soldier's coffins on TV when I was little kid, it was really disturbing. But here we are, still in Afghanistan, still in Iraq, and other parts of the Middle East nearly 20 years later. And we just sent troops to Saudi Arabia, which is a totalitarian dictatorship, ruled by false kings who torture and behead their own citizens. American wars apparently never end—as long as there's someone willing to pay for it.

Lisette: Knowing you as I know you Erin, you live every part of your life like a piece of art and it's very tangible. Everything, from how you wake up in the morning, do your spiritual practice, your martial art practice, your hair and make up—it's all part of the offering and the statement of your life. How does that feel from your perspective, and what is it like living your life like art, especially within the social justice perspective you've just elucidated? I mean, you are really walking the walk!

Erin: Thank you for your kind words Lisette! Well, I never looked at art as being separate from my life. The Catalonian artist/poet Joan Brazos said it best, "Art is life, and life is transformation."

I look at making art as being akin to breathing, or eating, or sleeping. It's a vital part of my life, which I have integrated into my daily practice ever since I was a child. And as far as walking the walk, in terms of social justice, the underlying statement of my work is about human dignity. Whomever I encounter, it is important that I treat them with respect, and that I am kind to anyone who enters into my orbit.

I think that is the most transformative act, simply being kind to all beings. The people I respect and admire most in this world are people known for their kindness, compassion, and empathy, which they embody in their daily lives. Life is not about worldly success, or wealth, or fame, or beauty, or celebrity. It comes down to how you treat the person who delivers your mail, or sells you vegetables, or collects your garbage. The day-to-day encounters and interactions between oneself and others—that is ultimately all that matters.

Lisette: I think that kindness is the greatest gift we can all give to each other.

Erin: I agree, and it's probably the most underrated yet most significant virtue of them all. Kindess is our most powerful and transformative gift to the world, and to each other.

And thankfully, it's a contagious one.

ERIN CURRIER

Final Thoughts

"The world will be saved by women." -His Holiness the Dalai Lama

I used to think that people like Septima Clark, Harriett Tubman, and Mahatma Gandhi existed out of the necessity of their times. That is to say, they existed in a moment in time, in history, when there was a real human need, and they happened to have that special thing that functioned to help them do what most others were incapable of doing.

This belief, by default, held that those of us living now, did not have the same opportunities to be great. But you see, I was wrong, and I think many of us have been wrong in thinking that these times call for nothing less than greatness. Somehow, many of us took for granted certain presumed rights and safeties during our time, even in the face of experiential evidence to the contrary, and we created a narrative that didn't credit us for our own unique strengths. I still see blatant racism, sexism, and classism in this world—countless lives have been taken senselessly by war, and even by our own police and security forces.

The US has one of the highest childbirth mortality rates in the worls, and one of the lowest literacy rates in the world—something is very, very wrong with the direction we are going. We must look out for one another, and support one another—the feminine power is needed in the world now more than ever. This is a time when heroes are born, when Buddhas walk the Earth, and we must live out our highest potentials.

The women in this book have all demonstrated an inner drive and a dauntlessness that has transcended their personal circumstances. They are certainly extraordinary, ordinary women—Poderosas all of them, but so are each of us, in our own unique ways.

The stories in our book highlighted three primary archetypes, those of the Artist (Visionary), the Teacher (Sage), and the Healer (Caregiver), but in truth, all of these women fit within the Hero archetype, as do Septima, Harriett, and so many others. The Hero transforms, and from that transformation comes an awakening, and then the Hero returns to save and nurture life. Which one(s) are you?

It is said that the Artist is the social innovator, the Teacher possesses deep and ancient knowledge, and the Healer lives in the highest service to others—they all understand that their own happiness comes from serving others. But it is the Hero, according to Jungian theory, that teaches us true mastery. Mastery comes from tens of thousands of hours of focused effort on the craft, so it doesn't matter if you shine shoes, clean bathrooms, paint portraits, or perform heart surgery—a master is a master, we are all needed, and we are all essential.

All the women in this book have personally graced our lives. They have nudged us along, making us better people with each turn, and our hope is that you will see yourself, and those around you, within them. We hope this may help you to rewrite your own personal story in a more empowering way.

Can you see the obstacles that you have to overcome, not through the lens of resentment, which only drains your energy, but instead as a piece of the puzzle to your Enlightenment? This is your life, a life that has made you stronger and better prepared for the world—the universe wouldn't have brought you here if you weren't needed! Can you bring down the borders around and within you, and move forward fueled by love? In the end, it is love that makes us mighty.

Each of the women in this book shared with us their personal story, but as we know, we are often perceived differently than we perceive ourselves. To begin with, each of the women in this book is a teacher and friend to us—and they are all heroes.

Carolyn Hartness, for example, married Barrett and I. She does not shy away from the problems she sees within the Native American communities, and she relentlessly advocates for healthier life choices, which literally saves lives.

Maria also works with Native American people through higher education, and she has helped protect and strengthen the Alaskan tribes from within, by using their own languages and cultures to do so. This also saves lives—and entire societies.

Magdalena, Edith, and the Shipibo Shamans are an example of Indigenous women who never left their homeland, and never veered from their ancient responsibility to carry on a lineage of traditional, Indigenous healing. They too save lives, both physically and spiritually.

Yuko and Angie are medical doctors, but Yuko gave up traditional medicine when she realized her true path—to cure all spiritual illnesses, which come from thinking we are separate from all things. She does this by teaching *The Way of Zen*, which is the spiritual nature of life.

Angie overcame cancer in her youth, but that process showed her the limitations of local medicine. She returned to fill that gap as a pediatrician, and now the children she treats have far better care. Angie and Yuko's work saves lives, both physically and spiritually.

Robin, a medical anthropologist who also overcame cancer, dedicated her life to understanding the cultural obstacles of getting the necessary medical care to women in need, as well as preventative care for breast cancer and HIV amongst marginalized women. She literally saved lives by helping women get the medical care they needed.

Miriam and Erin were born to be artists and activists. Their power is in their respective art forms, which is a passion for showing the struggle for human rights, while approaching it through wisdom, and the transformative power of love. I think many of us get discouraged from being artists because the path is so difficult and arduous—we are told to grow up and pursue something more profitable or stable. Both of these women have courageously lived their art and personal lives fearlessly, and in so doing, they become pure magic to everyone who sees their work. Without the arts, what would life even be? I would make the argument that art also saves lives, because it gives life true meaning.

Which brings us to our mothers, both of whom gave us life and helped shape our respective worldviews—perhaps we are their art projects. The relationship between a child and a mother is rarely straightforward, simple, or sweet. A mother has to plow through all that life throws her way, and somehow try to maintain a semblance of safety for her children. All the while the child is growing up from an idealistic version of their mother, into a more realistic, human version. How can that not be fraught with challenges?

I think motherhood may be the most difficult path of all. Our mothers gave us life, which is the greatest gift of all, and this power to create and carry life, whether exercised or not, is what makes women the wellspring for love from which we all can draw. Everything that happens after that is secondary.

When I think of lineage, be it familial, intellectual, or spiritual, I know that it is the feminine power that carries the wisdom forward. So for all this wisdom, and all its various forms of expression, I rejoice in these mighty women, these Poderosas.

Every person you pass on the street has a story to tell, so be curious, and never bow your head—walk like the mighty women that you are. Every woman can step into her power, or more aptly put, learn to step aside so that your power can shine through you.

Love yourselves, honor yourselves, so that in turn, the world can begin to recognize us all.

L. G.

FINAL THOUGHTS

ACKNOWLEDGMENTS

This book was the brainchild of my wonderful husband, and his musings on the impact of the feminine wisdom in his life. Together we would delve deep into conversations about the women who had changed the course of our lives, and how so very necessary it is for the pendulum to swing back towards feminine power. As he so often said, "Men have done nothing but make a big mess of things." This book is an attempt to rectify that imbalance.

It was a labor of love to literally travel from the Amazon Rainforest to the Alaskan Arctic together, and have the conversations that are included herein. This book would not exist without each of these women trusting us with their stories, nor would this work have come to a conclusion without the contribution of so many incredibly thoughtful and supportive people, including:

Barrett Martin took on the transcribing and editing of this book like a champ. Bear, you are a constant inspiration and not a day goes by that I don't feel your love, support, and respect. I never knew love and life could be so profoundly creative and generative. I thank you from the bottom of my heart.

Erin Currier is not only a world-class artist and the creator of the cover of this book, she is a next-level intellectual and spiritual warrior. Her feedback and support made this project all the more profound. Thank you Erin, for not only sharing your story, but for your friendship and love.

Chelsea Bailey, thank you for always being ready and willing to help. Your edits and comments on earlier versions of the book were invaluable. You are amazing!

To Robin, Miriam, Angie, Yuko, Maria, Gloria, Carolyn, Edith, Magdalena, Deana and my mother, Alma— you all are my heroes. I am so honored that you trusted me with your stories, and I am especially grateful that we get to share them with the world. May your stories elevate and inspire others the way they have me.

To Joy Harjo, who gave us some much-needed early feedback and direction on the outline and structure of the book. Joy, your contributions to the power of women is staggering, and you are, quite literally, a model to so many of us. Thank you, so very much.

To Juliana Um, for stepping in and helping with the cover design and layout of the book. You are a true gem, and I am eternally grateful for your generous assistance and your exquisite example of grace and kindness. Also to your amazing husband, Chadwick Shao, who put his touch on this, and other projects for me as well. Thank you my dear friends.

To Kristin Lee and Maria Kuolt, thank you for your business management acumen, and more importantly, for your belief in this project and everything we do beyond it.

To Carmen, Sarayu, Andrea, Isla, Rose, Angelica, Zoraya, Caelyn, Helen, Haley, Martha, Debbie, Adelpha, Amy, Senna, Kendra, Kimberley, Jaime, Roisin, Sherri, Nancy, Anita, Claudia, Jenny, Angie, Suzanne, Elizabeth, Sarah, Nicole, Irma… you have all inspired me in more ways than I can count. Thank you for your love, but most especially, thank you for your exquisitely unique example in the world.

Viva las Poderosas!

Lisette García holds a Ph.D. in experimental psychology from Tufts University. She has taught at Barnard College and Columbia University, and she later became a professor at John Jay College Of Criminal Justice. As a native of El Paso, Texas and the daughter of Mexican immigrants, her experience as a Mexican-American woman and human rights advocate has taken her to many different places around the world: As a civil rights activist who worked directly with Maya Angelou and Coretta Scott King, as an advocate for former child soldiers in Liberia, as a prisoner's advocate for the India prison system, and as a Buddhist scholar with over 20 years of practice and 4 years of silent meditation retreat. Lisette is also a percussionist and voting member of the Latin Recording Academy, and has worked on numerous albums in Peru, Brazil, and the United States.

Barrett Martin is a Latin Grammy-winning producer, composer, and award-winning writer and editor. He holds a masters degree in ethnology and linguistics from the University of New Mexico, he has guest-lectured at various universities around the United States, and he taught for 7 years at Antioch University in Seattle. His first two books, The Singing Earth (2017), and The Way Of The Zen Cowboy (2019) are about his musical work with Indigenous tribes and musicians in West Africa, Cuba, Brazil, the Peruvian Amazon, the Palestinian West Bank, Australia, New Zealand, the Mississippi Delta, and the Alaskan Arctic. As a producer, composer, and musicologist, he has worked on over 100 albums and film soundtracks worldwide. He is also a Zen Buddhist and martial artist with over 25 years of practice and study.

CPSIA information can be obtained
at www.ICGtesting.com
Printed in the USA
BVHW030750191120
593714BV00010B/48

9 780578 730882